Rose O'Connor
Footpaths

*love, adventure,
and finding home within*

Text Copyright © 2020 by Rose O'Connor. All rights reserved. No part of this publication may be reproduced, stored in a retrieval system, or transmitted in any form or by any means without prior written permission of Ms. O'Connor.

Published in the United States by Rose O'Connor, Chester County PA 19395

ISBN: 978-0-9985732-1-2

Original Artwork for cover design by Karen L. Hovde

For my traveling Joe — because of you

Table of Contents

Introduction 1

Colyton - Our housesit near the sea 5

Away we go 7
A romp with Roo 9
What it's like in the UK 13
Recharging with Reiki 16
The grand adventure continues… 19
Joe gets his beer 21
If you want to meet the locals, go to the pub 24
Under the brim of my hat 26
Making a home wherever we roam 28
Tell me a story 35
Welcome to the Polar Express! 37
What happens to us and what do we create? 39
The power of two 40
Another Reiki Master 44
A magical day 47
Still catching up 50
One sunny day 52
Christmas in England 55
A New Year ahead 58

Greenfield The New Year begins 63

Scratching the surface of me 65
In this moment 68
Our new sit 71
She writes 72
Quiet days, full days 74
Finding an opening 75
Tell me how you really feel 77
In the words of Liz Gilbert 80
Becoming a family 82
Day out! 83
Right mind 85
Who is my God? 89
New day, new deal 90
A different day altogether 93

February in Uppermill 97

What I'm learning in the UK 99
All in a day's move 102
Looking for the inside of Me 108
A month of writing 112
To see my soul light shine 114
An outing of my own 117
One windy Sunday 119
Another rainy day 123
Here comes the Sun 125
What I am learning through writing 129

The ups and the downs...	*131*
A break in the road...	*134*
Britain in July...	*137*
Let life happen...	*139*
Getting to know the neighbors..	*142*
All in a day's Sit...	*144*
How many ways can you lose a cat?...	*147*
You never know what you are going to get...	*149*
Time out with Felix and Isobel...	*153*
Moving through our last week in style..	*155*
Catching up...	*159*
My husband the Good Samaritan..	*162*
Anywhere; the world...	*163*

Huntingdon… a Short Break 165

A feathered nest..	*167*
A week in Huntingdon...	*169*
King of the Belgians..	*172*
Lunch in "Peanut Butter"...	*174*
Cambridge: a college town	*177*
Cambridge: Part Two	*179*

Scotland 185

Edinburgh	*187*
Edinburgh: Part Two	*189*
One more day...	*191*
Happy St. Pappy's Day!..	*193*
Driving Miss Mini	*198*
Berwick–Upon-Tweed	*201*
Everybody needs a Joe...	*205*
Two weeks in Scotland...	*208*
A house sitter's heartbreak	*211*
The road to recovery	*214*
Getting some perspective...	*216*
George and Greenie Beanie..	*220*
Parallel lives...	*223*
Important discoveries..	*228*
Don't be daft..	*231*
Why am I so happy?..	*235*
From Edinburgh to Thirsk	*240*
Flying back to the USA..	*244*
I am here to learn...	*245*

Author's Note 249

Acknowledgements 251

Introduction

Becoming a foreign exchange student at 58

Here I sit on a dark morning, per usual, in Colyton, England. It is December 2015. What I, combined with the incredible aid of the Universal energies, have humbly created here astounds me. This entire trip was conceived in my head and guided by the Divine.

Why do I think this was so? Because of the simple yet profound synchronicity of it all. Every step seemed to fall into place, without much help from me. First I spoke aloud to a class I was teaching this past April, hearing myself joke that I was planning to spend the winter someplace warm, like Mexico. Lo and behold, the next thing I knew we had renters for our home in Colorado.

Once the house was rented, it was a "simple" matter of where to go. I am a curious combination of dreamer and very practical person. I quickly realized that to rent a house somewhere else would probably cost us more than staying home. This was not the objective.

The objective was to get away from winter in Colorado and spend the winter at sea level. It was all over my vision board: pictures of my husband Joe and myself (or facsimiles thereof) on the beach, walking or riding horses. I even printed out the words "Living at Sea Level." There was nothing subtle about it; sea level was my goal. The year's vision board included 2015 and part of 2016.

I've been creating vision boards since 2011, and it never ceases to amaze me how much has happened when I look at them over time. A vision board is a tool to help you bring forth what you see for yourself in the year ahead. You use pictures and words to create a picture of what you see in your head and your heart. The very act of making one breathes life into your thoughts, and helps to turn them into reality.

What I learned this year in making one was that the Divine can and will deliver its interpretation of your intention, even if the specifications aren't exact! In my mind, we were spending our winter days somewhere warm and sunny, but I didn't put that part on my vision board; I just had pictures of us at the sea. So if you think of a vision board like a map, and yet on the map you don't have the correct highways or byways to get where you want to go, you may end up someplace completely different from where you intended.

Why was I so obsessed with sea level? Mostly because I was convinced that I would be healthier in all ways there—that I would breathe easier, lose weight, get some much-needed moisture for my skin, and most important, that my digestion would improve on its own and my hormones would balance themselves.

I've never been one to give any thought to aging, yet living at high altitude (our town is at an elevation of 8000') had begun to present some challenges. It was time to explore the inner workings of *me*. Always having an attitude of things having a way of working themselves out, I trusted the plan.

Another goal was to stay on budget while spending several months living elsewhere. So I joined a couple of housesitting websites, created a profile, and began to search. Though there were a few "sits" in places like Costa Rica, most of them were for long periods of time and some under adverse conditions, at least for us. It turned out, however, that there were dozens of housesits in England and Scotland over the winter. Could you blame them for wanting to leave the UK in the winter?

Housesitting is just as it sounds. You arrange a sit, talk with the person via Skype or phone, sort out dates, etc., and then arrange for transportation. In this case, no money exchanges hands. While they vacation, you simply stay at their home and take care of their animals and whatever other duties arise, such as picking up mail, taking out trash, keeping the place clean, etc. It seemed like a fabulous way to travel inexpensively and meet new people and their pets.

We were leaving the mountains of Colorado—a cold, snowy, but mostly sunny and very windy place—to go to the UK, which is a dark, cloudy, warmish, wet place—for four-plus months. The thought of being away in another country for four and a half months makes me feel rather like a twenty-year-old foreign exchange student. This is what they do, right? Except they don't leave a career to do it. In our case, it meant just that because we were about to put our Reiki business on hold for four and a half months.

I'm grateful to say I'm a Reiki teacher and so is my husband Joe. Reiki is a healing method for body, mind, and spirit. It greatly improves the quality of our energy and balances it, while allowing us to go deeper into our own selves—the place where all our answers lie. The energy that is called Reiki has been around for thousands of years and was brought into focus in modern times almost a hundred years ago by a Japanese man named Mikao Usui. It is fascinating that a healing method that is so easy and effective has continued to thrive and develop, especially in the Western world, since its rediscovery in 1922.[1]

Reiki relieves stress, eases pain, and has the ability to heal many physical ailments as well as mental and emotional ones.[2] It is used in many hospitals and hospices all over the world. I discovered Reiki in 2008, and it has become an integral part of my world—the world that has supported me intensely in many ways for the past three-and-a-half years. It's through Reiki that we met most of our friends in Buena Vista, Colorado, our hometown of four years, through teaching it or otherwise being involved with it. When we first arrived, we knew no one in our little mountain town. Reiki changed all that. We began to offer Reiki classes. People came. Friends were made. Our lives and the lives of others were changed by Reiki.

The story I am about to share with you here is about a journey—a journey of two people who, at the ages of 58 and 59, decided to leave their home behind just to find it again. We humbly thank you for sharing this journey with us and hope you enjoy reading our story.

---

[1] William Lee Rand, Reiki, The Healing Touch: First and Second Degree Manual (Southfield, MI: Vision Publications, 2016), 16.
[2] Ibid., 3, 10.

Colyton -
Our housesit near the sea

NOVEMBER 30

Away we go

As Joe likes to say, I go through life with head held high—walking straight into the abyss. Whilst flying across the "pond" towards England, I wondered what we would see, who we would meet, and how it would change us. The first stop on our housesitting adventure in the UK began in Northamptonshire, to visit our friends Nikki and Alex and meet their new baby, Henry, who instantly became the smallest love of my life.

I'd met Nikki almost 20 years ago when I managed a horseback-riding program at a summer camp in northeastern Pennsylvania. Nikki had come over for her first visit to America as a camp counselor, and she worked as one of my staff in the horseback department. She was 20 years my junior, but we found a friendship that has only grown stronger as the years have passed. She visited me many times in the US, and since she was now a young "Mum," it was time for the pendulum to swing the other way.

It was three days of fun and constant motion with Nikki and Alex as we followed them through their daily routine. Nikki's days included caring for eight-month-old Henry, 30 sheep, two horses, a pony, and two dogs, while working on her PhD dissertation and teaching college courses. Alex worked each day, making his living shoeing horses. In the evenings, when most men would be relaxing in front of the TV, Al would be outside at the forge, cleaning up or building something new, like a chicken coop, or getting things together for a new deck for their modular home. When Joe was there, they also shared a few beers and plenty of conversation at night, building a fire outside while Nikki, Henry, and I cuddled indoors. Nikki and I had five years of conversation to catch up on, and Henry proved to be a good listener, provided he was allowed to get a word in now and again.

The forge on the property is the old blacksmith shop, the original building on the property when they bought it. During days gone by, people would bring their horses to the forge to have them shod, but nowadays men like Alex travel around the countryside to all the different barns to do their work. For Al, working on the property they own is never-ending, yet it is a labor of love. He does most of the work himself, and loves finding bargains on materials and supplies for his different projects. Their dream is to build their own home on the property. Last year, when we visited briefly, he was working on a barn he'd built for the horses. Joe helped him finish the roof while we were there, and they got on famously. Alex said Joe was "alright for an American."

This year our visit went by all too quickly and soon it was time to leave them to begin our adventures with housesitting. We said goodbye at the station, embarking on our first of many train rides, this time to the Birmingham bus station.

Once at the station, we hauled our too-extensive array of suitcases to the bus. I'd named and categorized each one: Big Orange, Little Orange, Small Purple (me), Big Black, Medium Black, Small Black and the all-important Green Wellie Bag (Joe). Plus, we were carrying snacks and two Aussie-type rain hats, which would only fit around our necks or on our heads. What silly tourists we must have looked like, especially as we pulled, dragged, and otherwise lugged our travel companions with us from the train to the bus.

Here we began our first National Express bus ride, a long journey that took us to Exeter Station, where we met Grace, our first homeowner. Exeter is near the southwestern coast of England in a beautiful area otherwise known as the Jurassic coastline.

She took us back to her home a few miles from the sea, in the village of Colyton, part of Devonshire, where she served us a beautiful vegetarian meal of stuffed peppers and where we met the next-door neighbors, who stopped by for a pre-dinner drink. The company was pleasant, and I managed to stay awake through dinner, though we were soon ready for sleep. Tigger, the female yellow lab, and Roo, the black male, politely introduced themselves to us. Grace was set to leave the next morning for her month-long trip to Australia to visit family.

The house was large and rambling with low ceilings in the large kitchen, which once had been a garage. There was plenty of space for both humans and animals to stretch their legs, and there were three bathrooms, one with a lovely deep tub and two large bottles of bubble bath. I may be called a girl who likes simple pleasures, but not knowing what to expect either in accommodations, animals, or people, I was well pleased at the start of this sit. Away we go.

DECEMBER 5

A romp with Roo

Joe and I both love animals with all our hearts, and when I signed us on for these sits, I had visions of taking care of animals who were maybe just like the ones I'd owned in the past. But animals, like people, are all so different in their personality and way of seeing the world. This was a fact I was reminded of as we got to know Tigger and Roo. They were both great dogs though it took us time to get to know one another like any good relationship. Perhaps they were testing the housesitters, but to give them their due, they were both rescue dogs. I've come to the realization that one never knows what an animal has lived through, not unlike a person. We haven't walked in their "paws," so we can't begin to understand the composite of what makes them tick.

Tigger cheerfully climbed into the refrigerator every time you opened it, stretched out on the floor just under your feet whenever and wherever you were in the kitchen, and with unrestrained enthusiasm would drag you down the road when out for her walks. I think I should just put the leash on me instead of her; it would make things so much easier. The first day Joe and I took them into the village and got within whiffing distance of the butcher shop, we thought our arms were going to be stretched out permanently to match the length of our legs. Perhaps it had been too long since we'd been on the other end of the leash!

Tigger's owner impressed upon us not to leave ANYTHING out in the kitchen that was edible (or even something that looked edible). She wasn't exaggerating in the least. Roo, on the other hand, while seeming a bit more polite on the surface, was a relative newcomer to the household and hadn't gotten all the memos.

He was a beautiful black lab—my favorite kind of dog—with a lovely disposition, or so I thought until the first morning when I was in the kitchen and he grabbed a crumb-laden paper towel from my hand. I ran after him and tried to extract it from his jaws, which were firmly clenched. I carried on until he growled and showed me his teeth. Joe was about to reprimand him gently, but I said no, let him be. Best not to make enemies of a new dog straight away. The paper towel disappeared completely in about two seconds. Hopefully we won't see it again.

They do have very good qualities, as do all animals. Tigger is very loving and watches out for you when out walking. She pays attention and wants to learn. I still don't have a handle on Roo but I got to see a whole new side of him this morning when we decided to explore the seaside.

We'd forgotten their leashes, of all things, so we took them down by the river inlet on a footpath where we thought they could just run free. And run free they did. Tigger ran right inside the open door of the bait and tackle shop. No one appeared to notice.

After a short walk down to the water, or, in Tigger and Roo's case, a mad run, we realized I had a strap on my bag with snaps on it and Joe was wearing a belt. Leash problem solved, or so we thought.

We parked next to another footpath (a glorious feature of the UK – there's always a footpath!) that started along a well-traveled road into Seaton. As we prepared our makeshift leads to put them on the dogs, who were still closed in the boot, Joe asked me which eager dog I wanted to take. I chose Roo, having forgiven him for the paper towel episode. Joe tried to warn me to be cautious about getting him out, but his warning went unheeded. As soon as he lifted the lid of the boot (trunk), a black tornado leapt from the car as though it had been held fast for at least a decade, with me on the other end of my makeshift leash. I crashed onto the pavement face first, imagining that my head was right on the road that I just knew was filled with oncoming cars. When it comes to falling, my instinct is to close my eyes, not a great thing to do when you're flying through the air or trying not to imagine cars about to run over one's face or one's dog.

During these moments, Roo actually *was* loose in the road, and I knew cars were coming, but he managed not to get hit (this must happen all the time in the UK), and I was, as it turned out, still in the parking space, head and all. I felt so violated, my sense of quiet self completely and suddenly thrown, that tears came to my eyes. Joe was worried that I was hurt but miraculously I was not; there was not even a bruise later. I was just hurt on the inside and feeling put off by Roo, who, from his perspective, was just anxious to get on with his walk.

The sweet thing about it, though, was now Joe had taken up the black tornado and left me with Tigger, who, though she can full of energy, is very caring. As I reached for her, still in the boot watching the whole event, she stretched her neck to lick my face as if to ask if I was all right. She may not be perfect on a lead, but she certainly is sweet.

Off we went with our now-happy labs dragging us up a very steep hill for our walk. There are a lot of steep hills here.

Our daytime adventure is now just a memory involving sore limbs, and I am finishing the day with a long soak in a deep tub with plenty of suds and a book. Housesitting does have its perks. Sweet dreams, Tigger and Roo. Tomorrow your training (or possibly ours) starts in earnest.

DECEMBER 7

What it's like in the UK

Maybe you've never been to England, or perhaps you know it well. Either way, I will describe my own impressions as best I can. First, of course, are the differences in the way certain things are done or spoken about here in England. I find it fascinating to make my way in a new culture, even though in this case, the language is the same (though it doesn't sound at *all* the same sometimes). It interests me to think about going somewhere where the language is different and the way of life even more foreign to our own.

It's the little things that fascinate me. Take-out food is called takeaway and the showers are made here with just a half glass door, the back half of the shower completely open. The door swings open easily (sometimes too easily) back and forth, which makes good sense for cleaning purposes. You don't ask for the bathroom; you ask for the toilet. The food is so different and even when it is the same, the names might be different. Chips are called crisps and cookies are biscuits. I am finding it more difficult to find organic foods here and especially "clean" household cleaners and such. I suppose in the bigger cities you would have more variety, but we've been closer to the little village towns so far. Typical meals in restaurants are fish and chips, pies, ham and eggs, sausages of all kinds, loads of different types of fish. I have yet to see a salad on a menu! (Likely there's more to come once we actually eat out more often.)

We went to a village called Beer yesterday! A coastal village a bit bigger than Colyton, it sits by the ocean (or English Channel, as it were) with breathtaking views of the cliffs that jut out into the channel. The beaches here are not sand at all; they are covered with pebbles of varying sizes, making it difficult to walk on, especially in Wellies. Wellies, a rubber boot that pulls on and goes to the top of the calf, are part of our everyday attire as there is mud on many of our walks, and I mean *mud!* These boots are great and so easy for cleanup. Just a quick spray of the hose and you're ready to get muddy another day. It does take some getting used to walking in them, though. They are just plain rubber with no support of any kind.

The grocery store is so fun! We went to one in Seaton, the nearest sea town to us. Joe was in the car with the dogs, so I went in alone and didn't have time to linger as I might have liked. But all the food is so interesting; the cheeses so abundant and varied, and the lunchmeat is different in a good way. It is actual sliced meat, not processed, and they have so many things you don't see in America, like all the ways they make sausages and the little pies, etc. I love to grab things that are marked £1; because in my mind I think, "$1, wow, that's such a good deal!" Of course I know in my left brain that it's not a dollar, it's a pound. So, given the current exchange rate that's more like $1.50. But still… it feels as though I'm saving money on everything, and true or not, I like that.

The coastline in this part of southern England is called the Jurassic Coast with a sweeping wild landscape that is millions of years old. We walked a part of the coastal footpath that leads from Beer to Branscombe, but stopped partway through to go home to the pups. We will try to do the whole walk another day. Every bit of it is simply stunning! We climbed high alongside the ocean and could look back and see the nearby town of Seaton and the cliffs that extend from it.

And then there's all that green! I love the green; there's so much of it everywhere—green bushes and plants and beautiful gardens. Everyone has a garden. Everything is so rich looking and lush. *Lush* is a word they use lots. Also *posh*. My friend Nikki might say, for example if we are going to a nice restaurant with good food and service, that it's "quite posh." I do love the Brits.

In Beer, we found a fish shop down by the beach where one can buy fresh fish any day of the week, and they even deliver! After living in Colorado for five years, the availability of fresh fish, especially for a pescatarian, is extremely appealing. Back in the village center in Colyton, there is a small market, a butcher shop, a beer and wine shop, three pubs, a couple of restaurants, a post office, a tea shop, an old bookstore, a chocolate shop, a bank, and a few other places. There are no strip malls or shopping centers, just old authentic buildings surrounded by picturesque countryside.

The whole village center is about one block in a kind of a square. The streets are very narrow and in many places only one car can go through at a time, even though the street is meant for two-way traffic. When we walk into the village, we have to mind our feet, as there are places that wind around blind curves with no sidewalk. But the village isn't terribly busy, so even that's all good—it's all interesting and fun. Everyone walks here and everyone seems to have a dog.

The country lane that takes us to Seaton the back way, bypassing the village, is only wide enough for one car for about the first mile and a half, and it curves this way and that. When we come across someone coming the other way, one of you has to pull off (if there is a pull-off spot) or back up for passing. It is both fun and heart stopping at the same time, not knowing what's around the next bend. But Joe's doing a great job of driving.

He has been sick since we left Nikki's house and though getting better, he is still not his usual robust self yet. We haven't even been to the pub for a beer yet. Walking the dogs twice a day has been wearing him out enough, and I have been feeding him homemade chicken soup with bone broth to strengthen him up!

We made a reservation today for Christmas Eve dinner at a "posh" restaurant in nearby Colyford. We will get "cleaned up proper" and get out of our blue jeans and Wellies that night. All in all, it's promising to be a grand adventure.

DECEMBER 8

Recharging with Reiki

I'm becoming even more aware that energy exists all around me. I say those words all the time to beginning Reiki students. Yet learning is like an onion. There are many layers before you get to the juicy core, and sometimes you have to shed a few tears first.

My own vibration with Reiki is steady. Not earth shattering, not to me at least, just steady, grounded, solid and yet Light. I tend to forget sometimes how our vibrational frequency can be affected simply by places, people and events. We landed in our house-sit with high hopes for adventure, though tired from our journey. I expected to embrace everything in the manner that I do—especially when traveling someplace new—like a child with newfound eyes.

Yet instead I found myself tired, cranky, and even depressed and homesick. How is this possible? I'd only arrived in England a short time ago, and it didn't fit "me" as I know me now, as I know myself infused with Reiki's love. My internal Light had definitely dimmed and it was quite a shock, really.

It took me a day or two and then I finally mentioned it to Joe (who I'm sure had already noticed), and he admitted that his energy felt really low also and suggested that we recharge with Reiki. After all, we'd done a fair bit of traveling and sleeping in different places and, in our experience, sometimes one needs to clear their space both inside and out.

Though I'd filled our space with Reiki that first night when we lay in bed, I noticed that neither of us were doing our "routine" Reiki in the mornings. We were just slugging through the day, as it were. But once we spoke of it, we both began to consciously fill the place and ourselves with Reiki. One of the joys about being attuned to Reiki energy is that you carry the ability with you to use it at any time, in any place, for anything. Reiki can never do harm. I will repeat. Reiki can never cause harm. The energy of Reiki comes from the Divine, Source, God, the place of Oneness, or whatever word you wish to insert. This energy is all pure, all knowing, and infinite in nature.

As Reiki practitioners, we simply let this energy flow through us. Not from us, but through us, like water through a hose. Reiki is the pure, clean, sparkling water and we are the hose, the conduit for the energy. We can intend and allow this energy to flow through to anything, be it a person, an animal, a plant, an apple, or a house. It affects the energy of whatever it flows through by raising its frequency, raising its vibration to allow balance, clearing, and, if needed, healing.

Almost as though our intention alone started it, Joe and I both began to feel the shift.

I started to wake with a smile on my face and gratitude on my lips (which I most often do). I began the day with zest and plans and going a hundred miles an hour, as Joe likes to describe it. I like to think that I plan to wring the day like a sponge until I get every good drop out of it.

Today I realized that each time I clean a countertop or vacuum the dog hair or wipe out a shelf in the refrigerator, I can clean with Reiki, filling the space with cleanliness not only on a physical level, but on a spiritual one. The space itself seemed grateful, and I became more grateful in each moment.

When I came here to England, my plans were big… like maybe Reiki wanted us to spread it to others through classes or by giving Reiki in clinics—or who knows what. But this morning what Reiki taught me as I made a pot of soup was this: Right now, in this moment in time, my way to serve Reiki is to share it with this house, this town, the animals that live here and with my dear husband Joe. And nothing else is more important or "bigger" than that. What is most important in every moment in time is taking care of the vibration around us, and watching it ripple outward to the Universe.

DECEMBER 9

The grand adventure continues...

I am feeling more robust each day here and know that healing is coming through my body. The time in the mountains, while precious and ever ingrained in my heart, has taken its toll through oxygen deprivation. Here I feel my former strength returning as we walk three times a day. We walk the dogs in the mornings after breakfast, then go for our own adventure in the middle of the day, followed by an afternoon walk with the pups. My legs are beginning to remember their former strength (from horseback riding and Tae Kwon Do). My heart is soaking up visions of the sea and the beloved birds. Yes, seagulls and pigeons, but also great blue herons along the river, magpies, and beautiful tiny black and white birds whose names I do not know. I could look them up and know exactly what we humans call them, but I prefer to just look at them and appreciate their beauty and see my own within them. We are one.

I feel a communion here with nature that I haven't felt in the mountains; perhaps that is due to lack of breath there, or just a kinship of a different kind. Discoveries abound as I think of the vision board I created back in Colorado, in which the pictures showed us living by the sea. And here we are. Manifestation and I are in alignment.

After our morning walk, we left the pups tired and happy and drove to Axmouth, where the Harbour Inn boasted a large sign that said "The Breakfast Club," offering "Full English Breakfast daily from 9-11:30. 4

quid." Joe had the Hearty Breakfast for 7.50 quid or pounds ($11.25), which consisted of two fried eggs, sautéed mushrooms, cooked tomato slices, two strips of bacon (yum!) two sausages (double yum!) a piece of toast, and baked beans. My veggie option at 4 quid ($6.50) was one fried egg, mushrooms, tomatoes, beans, potato (like hash browns), and a slice of toast. I had proper English tea with cream and sugar cubes. The tea was the best part for me. I love English tea, but I only allow myself this caffeinated tea when we go out. It's the best. Joe met an older man with whom he could talk about hockey, so he was quite pleased.

I will, no doubt, start speaking with English expressions as we go along here, as it comes quite naturally to do so. Phrases such as "he was quite pleased" would be a British colloquialism, if you will.

We left the pub feeling content and drove down about a quarter of a mile to the town of Seaton for a stock-up on supplies for the house followed by a beautiful beach walk. It's a concrete boardwalk of sorts, and it fronts the town along the shoreline for a bit. The wind was bracing and cool, but felt so invigorating! The waves were different, as they seemed to have a lot more foam. We greeted many who were walking the boardwalk with us, stopping to chat with one man who walked with the support of two cuff canes. He was 99 years old and told us he swam the English Channel twice when he was younger. We found out that Seaton is a great place for retirees and that many people in this part of the country live to be more than 100 years old. Must be some well-kept secret. Maybe we should move there!

While I am a continual dreamer and my time here is so enchanting that I just can't squeeze enough into a day, Joe is still not well in himself. Though he's been a real trooper walking the dogs and taking me places (only one of us could be insured on Grace's car and we chose him to be the driver on this sit), he still has a cough and general lethargy, trying to get his sea legs as it were, or perhaps his English feet under him. He has taken two of our three usual walks today, and I think he will nap through the third. Sweet dreams, my dear Joe. I will be right here when you wake up.

DECEMBER 10

Joe gets his beer

Each day of the journey has a rhythm all its own. Some days are full, mirroring the weather—full of sun, wind, excitement, and movement. Others are slower, damper, cloudier, with lulls and dips and pauses. The tenth was one of those days. It was cold in the morning with the promised delivery of rain by nightfall, as one man stated succinctly when he was blown into the pub with his wet black lab named Angus.

"It's chuckin' out there," he said, making me grin. I had finally persuaded Joe that perhaps our good friend Larry was right: he needed to drink some beer to feel better. (Larry and I had been exchanging emails frequently. I was writing chapters for this book and sending them to him and his wife Sharon, so he knew full well that Joe was under the weather and had kept urging him to drink more beer for a cure.) Joe agreed, though I think he did it initially more for me than anything else.

So at threeish in the afternoon, we walked into the village to have a beer at the Kingfisher's Pub and Free House. Free, we came to learn, meant they are free to sell any type of beer. Though I still call Colyton a village, Bob, the bartender we met that day at the Kingfisher Pub, informed us that Colyton is, in fact, a town and not a village, since it has a public meetinghouse. This is the way they determine the difference.

There were three men there when we first arrived, and all of them were very friendly to us. The pub itself was a treat to our eyes; it was a real, proper pub, built in the 1600s. Inside there were low ceilings with exposed beams and stone walls. A wall-to-wall Persian-type rug covered the floor, and there were low tables made from slab side wood. The tables sat all around the oval bar.

On the bar was a photo of "lost pubs" in Colyton. One man who stood at the bar told us there used to be 13 pubs in town; now there were three. The photo showed the ones that were lost. I smiled, feeling the magic that is only felt by traveling – that of being in pure experience in a place very different from your home.

We sat by the snug fire on one of the low wooden tables sipping our beers and watching others arrive. Most of the men had a story about America, someplace they'd been or seen. The US sounded like one great Disneyland in their memories. Everyone wanted to go to Vegas.

Soon we were chatting with a lawyer next to us who was an avid fisherman. He urged us to spend a few days in London, though Joe protested (he doesn't like cities). He said it's the greatest city in the world and that his son works at Buckingham Palace—maybe he could get us in. I'm pretty sure he was kidding, but how neat would that be! An interesting man, he moved here from London to get away from working all the time and is now in a one-man office in the nearby town of Lyme Regis. He and

Joe shared fishing stories, while I started to feel a little strange after drinking a small, half-glass of Doombar, a type of beer originally brewed just in Cornwall.

Joe likes the 1664 lager; I don't normally drink much alcohol, but I am trying to embrace everything here (when in Rome), so I sip my half glass of beer slowly. But it still goes straight to my head! We looked at the menu and started contemplating food until Bob told us they don't serve dinner until 6. Lunch from 12–2 and beer all day and all night long. It was clear we weren't staying until 6 to eat; I'd have floated away.

The dog Angus and I got on very well, and his owner, Alex, a big man with a squarish nose and kind eyes, shared with me that he too had moved there recently to get away from the hustle and bustle. I feel truly blessed that we are spending time in a small place with lovely people and gorgeous countryside, not to mention being a few miles from the sea. Being here in winter is absolutely perfect, as I'm sure the footpaths would be much more heavily trafficked in summer. Even Joe being under the weather has its upside, as it keeps me closer to the writing. I *do* so much; getting me to sit still long enough to write is quite the feat.

Another man came in with his springer spaniel and sat at the end of the bar, away from everyone. I called to him, "Why are sitting there all by yourself?" to which Bob, the bartender, said, "Nobody likes him."

Bernie, one of the men who stood holding up the bar, told us that he had built the restaurant in the back, a much newer addition to the Kingfisher. We looked at the area politely, noting to each other that we would have to dine proper there one night, though I liked the bar better. It was cozy and had the atmosphere of old.

We spoke to the man sitting by himself on our way out. He reminded me of Ebenezer Scrooge: thin, long-limbed, long of face. His dog, a female, was whimpering and barking, and he said she always did that when he came to the pub. He swore that his wife had programmed the dog with a whining device so that he would come home sooner.

As we wound back through the village on our way to Tigger and Roo and a warm house (the heating was on a timer and would be on when we got back), I realized how amazingly blessed we are to have such an experience, one of not just visiting, but actually living in another country for a while. I'm sure we will be happy to get back to America when the time is over, but I plan to write the heck out of the experience in the meantime and be grateful for each day.

DECEMBER 13

If you want to meet the locals, go to the pub

So after a week of being here in Colyton, we spent our first few evenings at the pub, mostly so we could get to know the townspeople. Friday night, we sat side by side at a small table just next to the bar, where we could watch the comings and goings of the bar's patrons. A group of women dressed as Christmas elves gathered near our table to order drinks prior to their dinner in the restaurant in back. They told us they would be going round to different pubs for the next few weekends to celebrate. When Joe realized there were twelve of them, he named them the Twelves Dames of Christmas. They loved it! Friday was the busiest pub day so far.

On Saturday afternoon, we decided to walk back to the pub. The walk, always interesting, winds through the village. There are a couple of ways to get there and today we took the longer way that leads past the church and chocolate shop.

As soon as we stepped inside we saw our now "old" friend Alex and his dog Angus. He looked almost as happy as Angus to see us, and we met a new barkeep named Cara, who told us that she and Alex are both "blow-ins," which means they moved there from someplace else. Alex says that makes us "temporary blow-ins" since we're neighbors for just a bit.

Cara wanted to know all about our adventures in England—where we'll be staying and so forth. Everyone we speak to in Colyton says it's the best place in England, and it is grand, to be sure—a small town with friendly people and close to the sea. The surrounding land is covered with green fields and woods, and plenty of those wonderful footpaths for walking.

Sitting up at the bar, we met locals Charlene and Bob. We had a good friendly chat with them. Joe is in his realm here; he loves people and could chat with anyone for hours on end. He is getting right with himself again, getting his smile back along with the twinkle in his eye, so I feel better sitting beside him and knowing he's coming around. He took two walks with the pups and me today. Warm weather again. And deliciously muddy! We are getting our quid's worth out of the Wellies we bought, squishing in soft mud in the fields and sloshing through puddles.

Our mud dogs absolutely love it. Roo is a character in the fields. He loves his sticks and produces one every single walk, proudly toting it between his teeth. Today whilst trying to squeeze through a kissing gate[3] with his large stick in his mouth, he whacked Joe good on his knee, walking away undeterred while Joe rubbed ruefully at his pant leg.

It's an adventure a minute, even if it's just the Breakfast Club at the Harbour Inn or watching the sun finally decide to peek through the clouds for a half hour at the end of the afternoon.

We discovered a couple of new footpaths on our woods walk today, and one of the locals told us about a different town walk that we must try tomorrow. The country walks are amazing, to say the least. We are so blessed to discover them and there's just another and another, it seems. We won't even scratch the surface while we are here.

Charlene told us about Exmouth Beach, where there's actual sand, and where dogs can run loose in winter. I can see why people "blow in" here and decide to stay. It's a fabulous area to live in, even with cloudy skies and wet weather. This week, I shall try to figure out how to get us to see Poole, the town that bears Joe's name! Till then…

DECEMBER 15

Under the brim of my hat

This morning on our walk that turned rainy, I was grateful for the

---

[3] A kissing gate consists of a semi-circular, square, or V-shaped enclosure on one side and a hinged gate that swings between two shutting posts, and allows one person at a time to pass through but keeps livestock out. For more on this subject, see www.historyextra.com/qa/pucker.

Aussie hat upon my head. I contemplated the world as it appeared through the raindrops that hung onto the brim. The world was a sea, a very large sea of green. The only break in the green was the winding Coly River, which looked as brown as the mud I sloshed through. My mind wandered in time with my body as it moved along the river path. My life is always connected to one path or another. This one I'm finding rather interesting and different.

I commented to Joe how much my skin loves the moisture and the coolness of the mist as it soaked our jeans. He didn't comment so I assume he was just coping. Having lived the last three and a half years in arid Colorado, I hadn't realized how much I'd missed moisture. It felt soothing and healing to me now.

I thought about what I would write on this page when I got home from the walk and realized that I was grateful for many things this day: the rain, the mud, the dogs, Joe, being here in England, the very fact that I am able to walk and breathe, and I thanked my fingers for being able to type, to fly like the wind across the keyboard.

My friend Nikki brought how I type to my attention when we stayed at her home in Northampton. She said, "I would love to be able to type properly, like you do." Back in the Stone Age, otherwise known as the early '70s, there were two choices for us girls in high school. We could take the College Prep track or the Business track, the latter meaning they would prepare us to become good secretaries until we met our Prince Charming, got married, and popped out babies.

Seriously. And this is exactly what I did. I took the Business Course, and a few years after graduation from high school, I quit my secretary job to marry and have children, just as predicted. (In the end, I put myself through school many years later, getting my bachelor's degree at the ripe young age of 51.)

But three years of business training in high school gave me a skill I've been thankful for many times over—the ability to type, and it has stood me in fine stead on many an occasion.

I've read many times that it's best to do your writing by hand, pen to paper, to get the creative juices really flowing. I get that; I do. You need your soul to be close to the work. And I do write by hand but find that my words come much faster than my pen can keep time with, so today I am grateful for the fact that my hands can still fly over a keyboard, and for glorious rain that drips off the brim of my hat.

DECEMBER 16

Making a home wherever we roam

It's happening—an organic thing all on its own, and yet at the same time not without effort on our part. We have to continue to show up each day, with our brightest smiles and a desire to settle in. I am one who can adapt to change easily, having lived in many different situations, and yet I have a methodical side as well. As much as I like adventure and variety—different walks, different experiences, different conversations—I like a certain sameness too. Two of the things that you have to establish in a life being lived out of someone else's home is a place for things and a rhythm that works for everyone involved. Nonetheless, I am thrilled to realize that we are settling into our life here in Colyton as temporary blow-ins, and it's humming along very smoothly. We continue to enjoy ourselves immensely and find adventure in every day. One thing that's shifted in the last few days is Tigger and Roo. They have suddenly become much more responsive, more in tune with us, and because of this, we are reading each other's needs. I have begun to hear their language. An animal speaks to you all the time, if you but listen. I know when they want to go for a walk, when they are hungry, and when they just want affection. I've been making efforts to keep them more satisfied in their bellies, even though Tigger is required to stay slim due to her hind leg injury. That said, they are always ready to eat, these two, a trait not uncommon for most dogs, so I try to keep them happy.

We compromise and I give them a few more treats or carrots and a bit of chicken broth on their food (tomorrow morning they will get some bacon grease) and then be sure they run plenty so they don't put on weight. Roo I'm not so worried about, so I give him a little more here and there, especially when Tigger isn't looking. Yesterday I gave him the fat off the ham slice that Joe had for lunch.

They know I'm thinking of them, and they've started to respond in kind, working with us in a kind of partnership. Like us, they just want to know they are loved. They are responding much better in the fields when we have them out for walks, they are better on leads, and they are just as sweet as can be, really.

I think listening to Anna Twinney's webinar ("Animal Communication: A Limitless Language")[4] is making a measurable

---

4 http://www.reachouttohorses.com

difference and has come at a very appropriate time. Anna is a horse whisperer and animal communicator who works with people and animals all over the world. I met her a few years ago and studied bringing Reiki to horses with her, a passion that is flickering but hasn't come to a full flame yet in my life. However, Anna brought to me a true interest in the world of animal communication, and I decided to listen to her webinar during this month in Colyton.

As a result, I've begun to think that I can actually hear them. Body language, yes, I can pick up on all of that, but perhaps with more practice, I can also move toward becoming an animal communicator. My friend Nikki has always said that I am a natural horse whisperer—of course she is biased. But it's worth taking a look at, paying attention to. There's a whole world out there with animal communication.

That world is never far from my mind, it seems, here in England, where absolutely everyone we meet has a dog or two or three. It's hard to determine how many other dogs we've met out on our walks, especially through the beautiful fields we've discovered this week in town, off Rosemary Lane. I love the Rosemary Lane walks. They feel free and timeless. Rosemary Lane leads to a footpath that winds close to the Coly, with open fields and quaint country cottages to the right, the river to the left, and hills and valleys ahead. Every bit of it holds interest, whether the path runs quite close and is protected by trees or opens onto green fields. The energy of it holds a romantic and dreamy feeling.

Today was crammed full of movement and activity and fresh air, and our legs got a good workout. Right now as I sit on our borrowed bed, I feel as though I could jump back into a hot bath even though I've already had one this afternoon. We walked for miles today, starting first with our woods walk. This one we have to drive to, and going down the narrow country lane on a weekday morning around 8:30 or so was interesting indeed.

Today we passed a van, a lorry, and on our way back, a beer truck with our next-door neighbor, Oscar, driving it, and each time Joe had to reverse into whatever presented itself as a bit of a pull-off to let the other driver pass. They say doing something that scares you every day is probably good for you… but I must say, despite my jitters, that Joe handled himself really well, especially when I didn't "help."

After a good, long woods walk where we saw a strange white ball in the sky for a few fleeting moments (oh yes, we realized it was the sun), we brought the pups back to relax and dry out and then left them to snooze while we took off for Seaton and the sea. We stopped first at The Harbor Inn in Axmouth for the Breakfast Club once more. Today we ventured out of the pub area into a beautiful room with low ceilings and a massive stone hearth. This building dates back to the 12th century. This is where we chose to have breakfast, side by side, looking on at the fire.

Sarah, our waitress, was so kind, and she took our picture and didn't treat us like tourists. No one does, really. People are very kind, even those who aren't taking our money. She talks like my friend Nikki and called the full breakfast massive. It's interesting how quickly we've adapted to the different expressions, culture, food, and way of life here.

ROSE O'CONNOR

The sea in Seaton was out of this world. To quote Sarah, the waves were "massive," crashing up against the wall of the boardwalk. One time, the water sprayed so high, it covered the cement sidewalks and, as I later discovered, had washed up over the 20-foot wall and onto the cement boardwalk. As I stood by the ocean, the sound of the waves crashing was tremendous—I've never heard anything like it. I videotaped the sound to see if I could capture it. Being by the sea makes me feel so alive. I feel as though I could turn into a seagull and fly out across the waves…but, on second thought, with the velocity of that high tide this morning, I think I'll keep my feet down on the earth.

We did some shopping in Seaton after our walk. We always seem to find someone to have a lively conversation with along the way. This happens all the time here for two reasons—one is owing to the incredible friendliness of the people here and the other is because my husband can and will strike up a conversation with anyone. Hello or Good Day is never enough for my Joe.

I must admit it is the Divine's way of teaching me patience because I am one that always is apt to rush off to the 'next thing.' So I listened patiently while Joe and a man selling sundries in the post office discussed the state of the world and how to fix it, among other things. They finished with a brief conversation about sunny Colorado. The man told Joe and me that it would be pretty boring to live in a place that gets sun almost every day of the year, because he would never be able to put up his convertible top on his Mercedes.

We drove back to Colyton to find the pups eager for their afternoon outing, which was to start immediately if not sooner. This time the day had turned cloudier, so we donned our full rain gear, including rain pants. Boy did we look cute. It didn't rain on our walk today, however, and the weather continues to be quite warm, between 50 and 60 degrees. Another walk about 45 minutes or so in the fields by Rosemary Lane and we were home for a good rest and a dinner of leftover mushroom stroganoff and bacon from the butcher, with lovely greens for salad.

Speaking of leftovers, last night's dinner at the Kingfisher was a learning experience. "Be careful what you order" was my lesson. I thought all fish were just that, fish. I ordered something called blanchbait, which I thought was a mild white fish. It came out breaded and looking like little fries, tasting just awful, to me at least. Beware of any type of fish that has the word bait in it. I took another look at it and realized it probably was just that; bait for something else to eat, and that didn't include me! Joe tried one and didn't like it either, saying that it reminded him of sardines. But the bread and salad were good, and I shared Joe's stroganoff. We had a blueberry and apple crumble, which he loved. It came with ice cream, full cream, or custard and we got custard. The English do love their dairy.

We saw a man, David, who we'd met the previous Saturday night. He came over and shook Joe's hand, nodding to me, and said to Joe, "You're a friend for life." He's what I would call a proper Englishman—not stuffy, just very genuine with a reserved politeness.

So far here in Colyton, I've gotten the overall impression that the English are hearty, that they love nature and their animals, they hate the rain, and they love the pub.

For example, on our Rosemary Lane walk today, we met a British woman with a New York sweatshirt on. She smiled at us, hearing our accent, and was delighted when we told her that we were from Colorado. She wished us a good journey and said, "So sorry about the weather; it's just awful here!" I laughed and assured her that we get plenty of sunshine in Colorado.

Towards the end of our walk, I met another woman sloshing through the mud on the trail, and I told her, "It's great as long as you can stay standing," because I've wondered a few times if I'd end up flat out in the mud.

She said, "I'm not joking, I did just that the other day—landed right in it—and my husband looked down at me and do you think he asked if I was alright or anything? No, he just said, 'Well, you can't get in the car like that!' So I had to take off my pants and ride home without them. Luckily, I had a coat on that would cover me a bit!"

They are funny people. Between the accent, the way they express themselves, and their humor, I just love listening to them.

All in all, a very good day.

DECEMBER 17

Tell me a story

Yes, there is much to consider about our time here. If someone asked what has been the hardest adjustment, I'd say for me it has been the sudden realization that we've left our family and friends far behind. This didn't really hit until we left Nikki and Alex's house and came to stay here in Colyton. But I think that our initial challenge settling in here had a lot to do with Joe not feeling well too. It made the first week or so difficult on us both, but we got through. The power of two, as we like to say, is astounding, especially when combining our own energy with Reiki.

The other challenge I see is adjusting to the gloomy weather here, something that will follow us on our journey, I imagine. The thing that most surprises me about the house is just how old it is, and yet quite modern inside. (Though no hot tub, sadly. If there were I'd never leave the property.) But there is the nice deep tub in "my" bathroom. It's actually such a luxury for us to have two full bathrooms. Our house in Colorado is adorable yet quite small, with one bath, so it is a true joy to have a home one can stretch out in.

The bed in the guest room was very small and uncomfortable, so we moved to our homeowner's room (she said we were welcome to do so). Her bed is very nice, and there's a pretty view of the town from her bedroom window.

I like the upstairs better than down; the ceilings are low downstairs and there are no windows on either wall—just rear windows in the living room and front windows in the kitchen, which faces east. It's dark downstairs, especially on gloomy days, but much lighter upstairs, and you can see the tram from the guest room window.

I'm not too worried about settling in another place; I think it will be nice to move and be with other animals and in a different house by then, which is why I didn't want to do a sit for longer than a month's time.

The last few days have been quiet here. Tigger, Roo, the mud, and the cloudy days have been giving us a run for our money. Despite our intentions to go to the pub last night, especially after randomly running into Bob, the barkeep in Seaton, and feeling as if we now know people here, we both crashed after the afternoon sludge through mud. The locals say the ground is never like this in December; it is usually much colder and the ground is frozen. I'd much prefer mud and warmth.

That said, everyone continues to apologize for the weather. I figure it is part of the adventure and we are supposed to be here, well, because we *are* here!

In the meantime, weather and all else aside, I'm trying to build a creative practice of writing every single day here. I love my creativity. I love my creativity. I love my creativity. That's what Liz Gilbert tells us in her new book, *Big Magic*.[5] The more you tell your creativity you love it, the more it will show up! So today I'm riding on Liz's creativity! In fact, I shall sign off and go back to reading *Big Magic*.

This is one of the true luxuries I am indulging in here—lots of delicious

---

5 Elizabeth Gilbert, Big Magic: Creative Living Beyond Fear (London: Riverhead Books, 2016). Kindle edition.

reading and an equal amount of writing. I just finished books I and II of the Harry Potter series. I've never been interested in reading them before, but now that we are in England, it seems the right thing to do.

DECEMBER 18

Welcome to the Polar Express!

Tonight we took the Polar Express tram from Seaton to Colyton and back. There were adults dressed as elves, chefs, and of course the train conductor, and Santa waiting at the other end in Colyton. There were mostly children on the ride and it was so much fun to be a kid for a while. We saw Santa at the train stop, sang carols on the trip back, and had a blast watching a two-year-old boy named Archie who sat (or mostly stood) in the seat in front of me while his mum was on the other side of the tram car. Archie was a human balancing act, jumping up and down in his seat and defying the law of gravity, and yet the subtle movements he made to adjust himself were fascinating to watch.

Just in case, Joe and I encircled him, keeping our arms outstretched in his "aura" so we could catch him should he go flying. Seriously, even though his sweet young mother gently said from time to time, "Archie, sit down please," he literally stood on the seat and bounced up and down as the tram rattled down the tracks. Being on the tram and having to work at letting go and being silly and free, just like the children, made me realize how terribly stuffy and serious we become as grownups, and how much fun it is to just let go of inhibitions and be a child.

I got a bell from Santa's elf for Henry, Nikki's boy, and, for myself, a tiny pen that lights up and has a Polar Express train inside. I've bought myself a tiny notebook and keep it and the little pen in my pocket when we go out in case of sudden inspiration. *I love and honor my creativity* is my new mantra.

Later that night, we walked to the Kingfisher to eat dinner, and had to sit by the door for it was busy. Joe ordered pork, mashed potatoes, and carrots with peas and turnips and some kind of purple cabbage. It looked delicious. I got the stuffed mushroom appetizer with a small salad. An older couple named Doreen and Mike came in, and we invited them to share our table. Doreen has lived here all her life, she said, and never anywhere else. Mike is a wheelwright and makes wheels for the Royal Family by appointment of the Queen. Mike didn't tell us that himself; we found it out later from Georgiana, our neighbor down the street.

We talked with Mike and Doreen about the different customs for celebrating Christmas and New Year's.

"They don't celebrate Christmas much in Scotland but they make a big fuss over Old Year's Night (New Year's Eve)," said Mike. We listened, entranced. "On Old Year's Night everyone's house if open and you can walk into anyone's house and get a drink and they can walk into yours. And the celebration doesn't stop at midnight! It goes on and on through the night." He sat back in the booth, looking pleased.

Then he shared that here in Colyton on New Year's Eve, everyone gathers in the square at midnight. Doreen invited us to come by their house for tea one day (though sadly we never got around to it). As we walked home that night from the Kingfisher, the rain falling softly, little did we know that Friday was merely the spark of the weekend to come.

DECEMBER 19

What happens to us and what do we create?

Lately these questions keep coming up, although I believe I know the answers on some levels. We begin to talk about our experiences in life as though they have just "happened" to us. This or that went wrong. This illness caught us off guard or it didn't. So much of everything that happens we think just happens, as though we have absolutely nothing to do with it. It happened *to* us, right? "How could that happen to me," we ask?

Good or bad, pleasant or unpleasant, painful or deliciously sweet, everything that takes place in our life we have created in some way or another as a result of thought, emotion, or past experience. But try to tell us that when we are face down in the mud! Mud is a recurring theme of my life right now in the UK. I write this as the rain pours, creating even more mud.

Seriously, though, try to tell us how we create everything in our lives when the worst thing ever has just happened. We will stubbornly not believe it and will most likely try to blame someone else for it happening, be it another person, the weather, or God as we know her. That, dear friends, must be the work of our ego, yes?

And it is the same ego that wants to be in control all the time of everything that's happening in our lives; controlling and managing everything, planning and making lists. Then we become frustrated when something happens that we don't want. Perhaps it is the Universe telling us to pay attention to what we are creating. Where exactly do we need to "let go and let God" and how in the heck can we do that? Especially when we are holding on so tightly?

Everything in our life is altered by the thoughts that create the experiences that create the emotions that move into our physical being (our cells) that create us, that create the life we see around us. Things that happen to others around us may not have been something we created, but we are creating our future by how we react to and digest those experiences that others are having. Swimming too deeply for you yet? It is my own understanding at the present time (always learning) that everything shows up to teach us something, and if we can become *Receivers* of life and *Co-Creators* instead of *The One who is in Charge*, I believe the river will begin to flow in our direction and we won't have to paddle so hard.

DECEMBER 20

The power of two

In the world of numerology, the 20th is a 2 day, the same as my life path number. It resonates with me, and I usually feel quite good on 2 days, especially this one! The sun has decided to grace us with its presence today, and I can honestly say I have never appreciated it more. After two weeks of cloudy and rainy days (approximately; I've lost count deliberately), to see the sun has been just glorious—even if it has played games with us all day long, hiding behind clouds, and intermittently spritzing rain.

It's amazing what it does for the Spirit inside me. We went to the beach twice at my suggestion. The first time was to Beer after our morning dog walk and a breakfast at home of bacon and eggs (salad also for me and grapes for Joe). The bacon is killer here—which probably means it will kill you—but what a way to go! The sun was shining for at least 45 minutes when we got to Beer, and we walked on the beach and praised its presence fully, taking loads of pictures and watching the splashing of the waves against the rocks with the carefree spirit of children.

I love the frothiness of the water here; I guess it has been awhile since I've been to the ocean. And I love the ocean so much! I'm realizing that mountains don't do it for me the way the ocean does. I love all of nature, don't get me wrong, but the sea brings me alive. Maybe I was a mermaid in a former life. We took a short stroll through the village of Beer, and I bought some passion fruit curd to replace the jar of Grace's, which I polished off with deep pleasure. It's lovely on toast. We also purchased a jar of local honey made in Beer from free-ranging bees and a tin of Cadbury hot chocolate mix for my Cadbury-loving hubby.

We got an invitation this morning from our neighbor Georgiana to come to her home for a proper English tea at 4 p.m. today. After our morning adventures walking dogs plus walking in Beer, Joe came back to the house quite tired, as he'd been awake since before dawn. Although it doesn't seem as though your body has changed from living in a different time zone (seven hours for us), there are times when you just don't "groove" the right way, and I guess this morning was one of those times for Joe.

I made us some Cadbury hot chocolate (delicious!), and he lay down to take a nap.

After a while I couldn't resist the out-of-doors. The sun had come back out again! I ran downstairs, and Joe woke with a start. I urged him to please take us back to the beach—"Seaton this time, and with the dogs!" as it was close to their afternoon walking time. Joe, ever the trooper, put on his shoes and got behind the wheel (maybe not such a great idea since I realized after that he was still three-quarters asleep all the way to Seaton.) We made it with no crashes or bumps, parked by the inlet to the sea, and the dogs dragged us onto the beach.

There Joe had no choice but to awaken fully as the sea air felt brisk, the waves were crashing and the sun sparkling with a million little lights on the water. Magnificent. My whole being lightened enormously, and for about 30 minutes, we romped on the beach at Seaton. All along the beach were the white backbones of some kind of fish, and Roo loved chewing on them. Just as we turned to go back to the car, the sun ducked behind some clouds and surprise, surprise—it started to rain. Home we went.

By the time we drove the few miles home to the Colyton cottage, the sun was out again. Funny sense of humor, that sun today. Joe crashed for a half hour while I sat out back in the little grotto, typing until my fingers froze, content in the knowledge I'd wrung the sponge out of the day.

FOOTPATHS

A short time after, we left to walk two doors down to Georgiana's house for tea. So lovely! She had candles lit and her little cottage was warm and homey. She said her grandchildren called it old-fashioned, probably because the furniture matched the old style of the cottage, but I thought it very nice indeed.

We sat in her kitchen with her friend Freya and had a proper tea, which consisted of strong British black tea with cream and sugar served in pretty cups, scones homemade by Georgiana, crumpets, and little almond biscuits (delicious… all!). We hadn't eaten since breakfast so we tucked in with glee. The condiments included an array of butter, clotted cream (yum), jams, and peanut butter! A true British style feast.

We had a good chat and then Jennie arrived and joined us for tea. When we were out walking the other day, we'd met Jennie and a friend of hers on the Rosemary Lane path. Jennie had been wearing a great rain hat, and I had complimented her on it, which is why I remembered her so well now. I knew as soon as I saw her again that she was the sort of person I could befriend easily.

Jenny was funny and vivacious and I soon found out she loves horses just like me! She has an ex-racehorse that she uses for foxhunting, and she told me that she would be at the hunt gathering on Boxing Day at the Sea. Boxing Day, celebrated in the UK on the day after Christmas, is quite the holiday here and everyone gathers in Seaton to watch the blessing of the hounds and the start of the hunt from the seaside. She said she would look for us and that she'd be riding a chestnut horse and wearing a blue coat with a green collar, and that there would be only two people with a coat like that. She was funny and nice and was also a writer with a book about the walks around Colyton. She said she would slip two of her books into our mailbox for us to enjoy.

We found out about a farm store a few miles outside of our village, and Georgiana drew us a map to get there. We understood it was a bit hairy crossing the road to the store (heart in throat), so we will see about that, depending on how brave we feel.

After our teatime with Georgiana, Freya, and Jennie, we went downtown to St. Andrews for a service with the choir. The carols were marvelous and the old organ that stretched miles high to the ceiling was something to see. The church was over 1000 years old; that's really why we wanted to go. We simply wanted to witness something magnificent. It put a nice end to our night, and we walked home in the brisk air. The feeling of the grand church brought the spirit of Christmas into our hearts.

DECEMBER 21

Another Reiki Master

Such an eventful and fun week we've had. On Monday the 21st, we returned to our now familiar place, The Harbour Inn, where we joined the Breakfast Club (not a club, really, as usually it's just the two of us) and enjoyed our full English breakfast. When we arrived to sit at our favorite table by the huge open fireplace, a fire hadn't been laid yet. Joe and I were doing our best to stay cheery with the heavy weather upon us.

Two blonde cherubs soon brightened us up as they helped their daddy (named Gary) to light a fire. Gary, who is generally the cook, was off that day but came through that morning to light a fire for Holly, the barkeep. Gary's two little ones, around ages five and seven, kept asking him if they could look for Santa up the chimney. Gary lifted them sideways like a log, sticking their heads in the open fireplace (pre-fire starting) until they giggled and got a good look. They chattered away to him as he built a nice fire. No more peeking up the chimney now, he said with a grin. Gary is Sarah's partner, who is the other barkeep at the Harbor. Joe and I are starting to feel quite at home there.

With a nice fire lit, another couple who had stopped in for breakfast came to sit at the table just behind my view, and Joe started a conversation with the man named Rob. The woman's name was Judi and as soon as I looked into her eyes, something clicked. Everything she said was interesting to me, and we started to talk about diet and keeping healthy. She said she was 71 and I could have fallen off my chair in surprise. She was slender and looked bright and young, but without a lot of makeup or hair dyes and such—just naturally youthful.

As the breakfast time wore on, and we both finished eating, we took up talking again and Judi and I moved closer to hear one another over the cross conversation of the men. She began to ask about my life in the States and I knew, without a doubt, despite the lukewarm reception I'd been getting here telling people I was a Reiki teacher that Judi would understand.

In fact, I knew there was a reason to tell her. And, as it turned out, she too was a Reiki Master! We were so warmed by the connection. Judi told me that not everyone is very open to that sort of thing, even more so in the Devon area. This made me feel so much better, as I'd been feeling that I'd never meet anyone else with a similar connection. We could have talked all day, but eventually we both got up to leave and carry on our day, each of us reluctant to end our conversation.

Talking with Judi, however, absolutely brightened my day, and Joe was quite cheered by talking with Judi's husband too. As we cleared up the bill for our breakfast, Holly the barkeep suggested that we should come for Christmas Eve for the Ashen Faggot ceremony. She showed us the painting on the wall of the man with the big ash wood bundle in front of an open fire, explaining that it was a medieval tradition and great fun. She said that while the bundle of sticks burns, everyone sings carols and it's very festive.

In fact, only three pubs in all of England still honor this ceremony and the Harbor is one of them. We were hooked and later that day decided to cancel our dinner reservations at the place in Colyford for the posh dinner and have pub food at the Harbor instead, staying on for the Ashen Faggot starting at 8 p.m.

It cleared a bit, so we took a walk down on the beach at Seaton. We love walking on the cement boardwalk and no matter the weather (usually quite brisk), I always feel so refreshed and alive after doing so.

We came home to another dog walk and a quiet end to our day, making phone calls to home. This area of Devon is becoming quite dear to us, and we feel we could easily return to explore here again. As people have told us, this is old England and perhaps why we've not met any other tourists. Everyone we've met lives locally or someplace else in England, and we've become such a part of the landscape. We've begun to see the same people on our walks —Charlie with his two black dogs, Sophia with her motley crew, and Freya, the shy woman from our tea, with her dogs—among others.

The sun goes in, it rains, the sun comes out, the wind blows; it's all the same. People walk their dogs through the glorious fields on the footpaths laid out for all. We pick up other people's dog poop bags on our way back to the bin, and we share the land with one another—the land, some conversation, our dogs making friends—trading sticks and their own stories. People are so friendly and genuinely warm here. Kind, respectful, interested. Most of them seem to have a good way of looking at life, of carrying on. They aren't mushy or much on hugging and such (their way is a kiss on the cheek instead), and yet there is a warmth about them to be sure. It's a grand life.

DECEMBER 22

A magical day

I love the 22 day even more than the 20. It's a double 2, and 22 is a Master Number. I continue to send Reiki to many situations, not the least my dear friend Nikki, who is five hours away with a hurt back. She has had her share of it lately, to be sure. Among others, we are also sending Reiki to Joe's Mom and Dad back home in Pennsylvania. Reiki knows no time or distance. The Divine energy of Reiki can be sent to situations across the world or across decades. A difficult concept at first for people to grasp, Reiki helps those who practice it understand we are all connected.

It's a partial day off from pet sitting for us, and we started with a Tigger/Roo walk, per usual, followed by breakfast at home. I managed to cram a lot of chores into the morning, and we left by 11 to go to Sidmouth, another town along the Jurassic coastline. What a place. We parked at the beachfront and began our walk to see a place called Jacob's Ladder (recommended as a good lunch spot by Grace). The beach was WILD at Sidmouth! The tide was working its way in, the day was cold and windy—so windy that I could hardly keep my hat on. We got directions from the ticket keeper at the car park, a great grinning fellow. He pointed us down the coast towards the cliffs, saying, "Down that way a bit and up the hill."

Unsure of where we were headed, we were blown along the wild shoreline, finding a path that hugged the giant red cliffs with signs advising us to watch for falling rocks—which of course made me ever so reassured! The weather was fierce, the waves came a'crashing, and we knew not where we were going or why. Along this lonely road, we met a man, and Joe asked, "Jacob's ladder?"

"Yes, yes," he said, "keep going." We couldn't see around the cliff bottom, with the only view being of more rock, more turns, and more sea splashing. I wanted to turn around but Joe forged ahead, confident that we were in fact going to Jacob's ladder. Finally we reached a clearing on the other side of the cliff wall, and a couple pointed to a white wooden staircase, saying yes, that is Jacob's ladder and yes, there is a restaurant at the top of the cliff.

I have never been a fan of ladders nor great heights, but up we went. And at the top was indeed the Clock Tower Restaurant, an ancient building made of stone with tiny windows at which you expected Rapunzel to appear at any moment.

I felt as though I had indeed walked inside a fairy tale as we entered. The bake shop and place to order was downstairs and the winding steps led up to the tower, which was fashioned with tables and chairs for eating and peeking out the crystal-shaped windows to the sea far below.

We weren't ready for lunch so we ordered a pot of tea and a scone to share. The experience was enchanting. After we walked through the gardens next to the clock tower, we discovered a proper road that led back into town, past grand Victorian mansion hotels. Sidmouth is, on every level, much grander than any of the sea towns we've been in so far and reminds me a lot of the movie "Somewhere in Time," with its same sense of beauty and grace.

We walked downtown to find Fields, a department store that we'd been told to visit. It was very large and had just about everything. On the second floor was a cute little cafe where they served all manner of sandwiches and every proper kind of tea complete with simply scones or scones, crumpets, cheese, and a pickle. Joe ordered a tuna sandwich and I, a Rose Prawn salad. Everything was delicious and, like the tea, we had very proper service, with the waitresses dressed in white blouses with black bow ties. It was all quite posh but also friendly and down-to-earth at the same time.

Afterward we whizzed up the hill in our little British car to find the coveted Waitrose supermarket that our homeowner told us about. Less than impressed with the crowds, we finished as quickly as we could and came home to find that Sarah, the woman who was covering for us that afternoon, had already walked and fed the dogs, so we could sit back and relax for the rest of the day.

What a great day! We were both feeling healthy and refreshed by our time at the sea and all our adventures. We had even bought a few cards and a gift for Sue or Georgiana, who may possibly take us to the bus station next Wednesday, and a small gift plate for Grace that had a picture of two labs on it that looked just like Tigger and Roo. Happy days and long nights!

DECEMBER 23

Still catching up

Journaling about our trip is teaching me about "the moment"—the moment that something happens, for instance, is when you should journal it. Somehow when you wait a day or two and look back, the emotion of that time is harder to catch again. The magic is there and then it moves on, just like the energy.

Yet I will attempt here to recapture the feeling of December 23. We woke to miraculous blue sky (okay so it was light grey, but it wasn't raining and there were no clouds), and we were both anxious to grab hold of the day. We walked Tigger and Roo in their favorite horse field (now missing its horses), where they've found a new pleasure that involves rolling in dead fish stuff in the field. Heaven only knows how the fishy stuff got there in the first place. This perfumes them up so beautifully that we then have to throw a stick in the river to wash it off (all part of the grand adventure!). These dogs don't like being bathed, so to the river they go. Luckily the river Coly runs right alongside the horse field.

After bringing the dogs back home, toweling off the mud and giving them a biscuit, we didn't even want to stay inside long enough to eat our breakfast, so we took off for Seaton to walk along the water. But by the time we got to Axmouth (which is on the way), Joe was getting a headache. So we stopped at the Breakfast Club for our usual English breakfast of egg, grilled tomato, mushroom, hash browns, and toast and beans for me, sausage and bacon for Joe. While we were there, Sarah booked us the perfect table for watching the Ashen Faggot ceremony on Christmas Eve.

Seaton was very blowy and just gorgeous, and even though the clouds had come in, we could still see glorious sun! We walked about the town, deciding to treat each other to a Christmas gift. Joe bought a pair of flannel pajama bottoms and a very warm pair of socks to replace his hole-filled Smartwools. I think we will have to go back and get him a few more pairs, as he discovered he really likes them, and they are good value (£6). After much deliberation, I bought a Tilley hat, just like my horsey friend Jenny was wearing the day I met her. It's wool but waterproof, warm but light. You can crush it and put it in your pocket, and it's washable and guaranteed for life.

In the Tilley shop we met Liza (pronounced Leesa), who was grand and very talkative. She rides horses, owns five Tilley hats (!), and knows about Reiki. She and her mum are part of a franchise to sell these little metal tags that go onto dog or cat collars that emit frequencies to keep fleas and ticks away. I'm sure this isn't new, exactly, but it was great to find someone else with whom we could discuss our work with Reiki. We talked about Nikola Tesla, who understood quantum physics and the laws of energy long before his time. Great stuff and good conversation!

We tested out the Tilley by walking along the sea once more to see if my new hat would stay on my head in a brisk wind, and it did. After driving back to Colyton and having another great walk with the pups, we felt a good tiredness, and very well aired out! I can see why people here live long and healthy lives by the sea—lots and lots of walking and plenty of fresh air.

DECEMBER 24

One sunny day

This morning, Christmas Eve, started blustery and rainy. We walked Tigger and Roo only as far as the first field and then we all scurried back to the house. Still wanting to be in the adventure of the day, rainy though it was, I asked Joe to take us to find the farm shop that Georgiana told us about.

It was raining a lot when we left, and Joe was none too happy about exploring back roads in the washout and not knowing where we were going. I must confess to doing a bit of side-seat driving that didn't help matters any. We wound our way up a steep hill, through a village or two, and finally out to a gas station where I asked directions and got more confused since we didn't even know the name of said farm shop. Directions from people here can tend to be on the order of "go past the big oak tree, turn left at the old mill, and then it's a bit down that road."

When I got back into the car, Joe said he thought we should return home, but I was now determined. "Please? One more try? We've come *this* far." He reluctantly agreed. We drove back to the village where we thought we'd missed the turn and drove up that road for what seemed a long way. Seeing a car on the side of the road, I jumped out into the rain to ask the man about the farm shop, and indeed we were on the correct road. Good thing we got some confirmation, as we drove ever farther and farther it seemed, but suddenly there it was, the much-talked-about farm shop! It was named Taylor's, after the owner.

The only thing I could think of when we were walking around the store was that I wished we would have known about it three weeks ago. We could have done all our shopping there, as they had fresh baked bread and croissants, all manner of nuts and seeds, ham, bacon, and other meats, fresh farm eggs, and loads of fresh veggies. The selection was much better than at the local stores and somehow looked so much more appealing. Even though we don't really need much food, since we are leaving here in about five days, I bought several things just because I couldn't resist.

Joe and I get along so well and yet we are hardly ever thinking about the same thing (must be a Mars/Venus thing). As my mind was stirring with thoughts of gathering delicious healthy food for us, Joe was thinking about the five-pound note he'd found in the parking lot. He was very excited about finding it and carefully dried it with the blow dryer when we got back home. Joe's always been great at finding money and did it for many years when he lived in Pennsylvania, donating it all at Christmas to the Salvation Army. Ironic that he finds a five-pound note in the UK on Christmas Eve.

On Christmas morning when we walked the dogs in the horse field, we saw Oscar, our next door neighbor, and he told us a funny story about Mr. Taylor, the owner of the farm shop. He said that Taylor was a farmer who got lucky when he opened the store years ago, and people came from all over to frequent the store. He got very rich, so rich that at one point his accountant told him he needed to spend some money.

Oscar describes this guy as a man with holes in his overalls. He told us about the time that Mr. Taylor had walked into an Aston Martin's car dealership… in his farm clothes. He picked one out and told the man that he wanted to buy it, laying £130,000 on the table in old bills. That same car sits in his barn because he never drives it. Oscar says he's afraid to. Once a farmer always a farmer I guess.

Once we finished at the farm store on Christmas Eve morning, we came home on rain soaked roads and devoured a large snack from our purchases. I sat down to catch up on my journaling and—wouldn't you know—the sun came out! The day turned completely around. Joe couldn't wait any longer and so he took off with the dogs and I met him in the fields a few minutes later, where he had met up with Emily (married to Alex from the pub) and their dog, Angus.

After our walk, I took a long nap even though bright sunshine poured through the window. It was probably the brightest day we've had. I just couldn't "go" anymore; this energizer bunny needed some recharging before our much-looked-forward to Christmas Eve dinner at the Harbor. Once we got there, we had flatbread pizza and shared part of a bottle of wine.

We waited a long while for them to lay the branches in for the Ashen Faggot as the place began to fill up, mostly with people just there for the ceremony. Prior to the start, the owner and another man read a poem and explained the history of the Ashen Faggot ceremony. Then they laid in the big bundle and the two of them sang two beautiful Christmas songs, ones I'd never heard before. They handed out sheet music and everyone sang while the bundle burned.

It got very smoky, and so I backed out to go to the ladies room. While I was washing my hands, I heard smoke alarms going off all over the restaurant. I wondered if people would be shuffling out, but no, everyone was laughing and drinking and singing while the alarms continued and the staff scurried to turn them off, which amused us both. The bundle burned down quickly and Joe and I left soon after.

A great night in a great place. Happy Christmas Eve to all.

DECEMBER 25

Christmas in England

The day of Christmas was quiet for us. We took Tigger and Roo to the horse field in questionable weather, though it wasn't chucking rain yet. We met Oscar out walking his dog, and he told us to come by the pub for a pint at noon. The pub he frequents is the Gerard Arms, not the Kingfisher. He says it's less expensive and more of a local's spot. "Me and the lads will be going for a pint, as the wives will be kicking us out of house to make the midday Christmas meal. Join us for a pint."

Most interesting on our walk, Roo decided to take a big swim in the Coly. Usually he jumps in for a splash and right out again, but today he just kept swimming. At first we thought the current was too strong and he couldn't get out, but when Oscar showed up he said, "Oh, he's alright, he's just having a bit of a swim." Roo stayed in the water for at least ten minutes, at times diving under. Oscar called him an otter, and indeed, he quite looked like one! We stood and talked and had a laugh with Oscar until finally Roo emerged, dripping wet.

The three dogs all ran and played as we walked companionably together to the end of the field and back, at which time Roo decided to roll in his fishy spot again. So once more back to the swimming hole for Roo and Tigger, promising Oscar we'd see him later.

The morning passed with each of us doing our own thing in the house, while it rained and blew outside. Around 11:30, we couldn't decide if we really wanted to walk to the pub so I told Joe I'd soak in the tub and we'd give it a bit. After a hot soak I was ready and raring to go again. I tied my Santa bell (Henry's Polar Express bell, actually) on a ribbon around my neck for a bit of festive spirit and then found Joe on the couch napping. He woke up and I said, "Well, from the looks of the day we've got plenty of time for napping so let's go have a beer at the pub and meet Oscar for a bit." He agreed. Joe is always game.

The weather outside was not bad at that moment when we walked over to the Gerard Arms down Rosemary Lane, a familiar path to us both by now. The Arms was packed with people laughing and greeting one another. Soon inside, we saw tall Oscar at the bar waving us over and buying us each a pint. He introduced us to his son Jim and his daughter's boyfriend, plus we met a man who used to live in the house where we are staying for seven years before buying a beautiful thatched cottage out on the moor along our

Rosemary Lane walk.

I've admired his cottage every time we've walked the fields beside it, as it is set really nicely along a country road with an attractive piece of fenced ground around it. It's just an ideal old English cottage, though a good-sized one at that.

After Oscar and Jim left for dinner, we saw our new friend Charlie, from our dog walks, and his son-in-law Rob, and they came over to talk with us awhile. Rob is a landscape architect who works locally for universities and such. Charlie, a former butcher who retired at 45, has the black dogs we see a lot on the Rosemary Lane fields. We had a great chat with them and Charlie told us how much he loves Las Vegas and that he's going again in 2016.

The English love America, and we told them about driving for miles and miles out West without seeing a soul. When I told Charlie that we drive to Idaho and that it's an 800 mile drive from Colorado, he said that the farthest place in the UK, up in Scotland, was as far as he could drive in this country, and it was less than 800 miles!

The next day was Boxing Day, and Joe and I drove to Seaton to watch the hunt take off along the beach road. Droves of people came to watch. We walked up a steep hill to view everything from above, and the hunt rode up the hill past us. We took pictures and I made a video to capture the clop clop sound of the metal horseshoes hitting the road's surface.

On the way back down the hill afterward, we saw the swimmers in the sea for their Boxing Day swim, another tradition in which people dress in fancy dress and then jump into the freezing English Channel. It is all done for charity and a bit of fun. The wind was out in full force today so I can only imagine how cold those swimmers felt. We enjoyed a walk along the boardwalk in communion with many others out to enjoy the holiday.

Back home we came, happy and exhilarated from our adventure to have a rest before the afternoon walk with the pups.

DECEMBER 29

A New Year ahead

After our morning walk yesterday, we got a call from our homeowner Grace, saying she would be at the Axminster station two hours ahead of schedule. Tuesday began as a gloriously sunny day, and we both realized that it had been a while since we'd seen the sun. It felt so very, very good. On our way home from the station, Grace kindly suggested that we take her car and go off for the afternoon, which was a very thoughtful thing for her to do.

We set off for the village of Branscombe—there's still so much of old England in this part of the country. The drive there was a hair-raising adventure: another long and twisting downhill ride on a narrow road built for one car, not two. The Mason Arms, where it was recommended that we go for lunch, was one of the first buildings we wound past through the village of turns, houses built right into the curves, or vice versa. Finding nowhere to park that was obvious, we followed the signs a half mile to the beachfront and car park. The views of the Jurassic coastline were spectacular—and it was windy. As usual.

We strolled the beach, then walked the footpath back up the hill to the village pub. Great walking alongside the fields of sheep and green, and it was a popular path.

The Arms was a beautiful old pub that was packed with patrons. We found our way through the crowd cueing up for a pint and ordered sandwiches and pints, then went to sit at an outside table. Imagine at the end of December being able to sit outside! It was cool but just so appealing. Joe got a chicken sandwich with lemon mayo, and I ordered a cheese and chutney sandwich with a bag of cheese and onion crisps. It came with a nice small salad and coleslaw, and the beer was delicious! The Tribute Ale is my favorite as it is very light.

After lunch at the old pub, we walked back on the path to the ocean and decided to climb the big hill that overlooked the sea and led along the coast path to Beer—a walk we agreed we must come back and do another time. There we found a nice place with summer cottages to let. I imagined bringing our good friends Larry and Sharon here and spending a couple of weeks looking at the sea in Bournemouth. We sat down at the beach until the rays of light started to fade and it became cool. It was a moment for me that could have lasted forever. So content, so completely alive.

Back to Grace's place where the pups, now our good buddies, greeted us enthusiastically. Grace thanked us for taking such good care of her dogs.

She said she could see how happy they were, and they weren't even bothered about her coming home at all. The next door neighbor Lucy invited us over for a drink after dinner. It was a fun visit with Grace, Lucy, Oscar and son Jim. We sampled beer from the brewery where Oscar works and gets free take-home beer each week, snacked on cheesy bread and crisps that Lucy set out, and listened to stories of Lucy's police career, which is how she and Oscar met.

Oscar showed us an old Billy club and sword that they'd inherited from an uncle. We talked about all the places in Europe they loved to go, and I asked them which place they would choose if they had just one place to visit for a few days. Lucy said Paris definitely, despite the recent bombings. Oscar said you can be there in a blink. My friend Nikki had suggested Bruge in Belgium for a weekend, which Lucy also thought was very nice. Grace said she would choose to go to Venice or Rome.

The conversation shifted to pub talk. After all, our gathering was similar to what people go to pubs for—to have a drink and socialize. Jim stated that the iPhone was the death of the pub discussions that used to last for hours as people sipped beer and talked about one thing or another. That gave me an idea. "Why don't we discuss something as if we were back in those days? The days before people in pubs had iPhones?" The others looked interested. "I've got a pub question for you. What percentage of Americans own a passport?"

Numbers were thrown out and everyone had a vote. Jim pulled out his phone (death of the discussion) to confirm that in fact 40 percent of Americans have a passport but only three percent actually travel abroad.

It was a fun evening and back in Grace's house sleep came quickly as did 4 a.m. when the dogs had to go outside. We all were up by 6 and off to the bus station by 8:15. Prior to our departure, however, Grace suggested a sit and cup of tea. She said her mother used to make them sit on their suitcases for 10 minutes before they went anywhere. Just sit first, she would say.

Grace gave us the magic number to call for train tickets. She says it's a lot cheaper than booking online, so we will try that next time.

Our journey today, December 30th, is a long one. We've been on the bus for almost six hours but are getting close to our destination: A lovely stay at the little rented cottage to bring in the New Year with Nikki, Alex, and Henry. We can't wait to see them. It's been a month. We will leave more of our things with them and lighten our load for the next journey. Silly Americans, we have to learn the hard way round. More is not always better.

Greenfield
The New Year begins

JANUARY 3

Scratching the surface of me

It was just perfect spending time with Nikki and Alex over New Year's. The bus ride back to Northampton was an experience. We drove through London "town" down Buckingham Road and into Victoria Station after a four-hour journey in which I read, Joe napped, and we ate peanut butter and jelly sandwiches. Victoria Station held a collection of every nationality. It's strange after living in a small, white bread town in Colorado to suddenly be thrust among all types of people. This is the real world, unlike the one that we live in. This is a world where people are vastly different and interesting but where there is also ugliness: crime, poverty, and the like. I find this world jarring to my delicate system. I realize that my insulated existence is much more palatable, but it is just that. Insulated. And because of my work with Reiki, I must be willing to experience all of it—the beautiful and the not so beautiful, and see the Light that weaves through it all.

Two and a half more hours on another bus and at last we reached Nikki and Hen in her new (used) Land Rover with rain chucking down. She dropped us off at our cottage across the road. Henry was crying in the car, which is so unusual for his happy self. But his tears turned to smiles when he saw our new place, decorated for Christmas with lights and a little tree that Judith, the innkeeper, had put up for us.

The cottage is adorable, just lovely. It has a cozy living room with a wood stove and dining table, a snug kitchen complete with dishwasher,

washer, and dryer. Our bedroom is quiet and comfortable with its ensuite bath, complete with one of the deep tubs I am coming to love so much. Sleep came swiftly.

On New Year's Eve, Nikki and I sat inside their home and talked for hours, with Henry sleeping in the next room. We made ourselves a "tea" with cheese, crackers, grapes, and smoked salmon, and drank a bottle of rose lemonade while the guys hung outside by the fire and played darts. It was easy to see that Al was enjoying Joe's male companionship, and we waved to them through the window of the little modular from where we could see them clearly standing by the fire and wearing funny New Year's hats. For me, I was quite happy to stay warm inside with Nikki as she watched over her precious Henry. She is thrilled to be a Mum and is very good at it.

The lights in the old Rover, which Al is letting us use to go back and forth to the cottage, aren't working, so Joe and I elected to walk home just before midnight. Nikki gave me an extra jacket, and I used my phone for a flashlight. We rather enjoyed the mile-long walk back in the night, past the cows snoozing in the fields, while watching the stars give way to fireworks just as we reached the cottage. We watched the New Year roll in from our window as we talked to our cousins from home.

The next couple of days flew by. We had a really delicious lunch out with Nikki and Henry the last day before leaving for our next sit. We said goodbye to our little cottage and it bid us farewell with a beautiful sunrise on our last morning. I ran out onto the wet grass to take pictures and celebrate the sky. You don't see it every day here. Some days it's just grey and clouds. And yet everything about this trip makes me appreciate my life more in all aspects.

Our next transport was via train, and it was a short trip this time. Just 40 minutes to meet our next homeowners, Jacob and Jill, and their two cocker spaniels, Biscuit and Molly. Luckily for us, the third spaniel, the so named troublemaker Poppy, had gone to stay with their daughter.

This sit is in some ways much easier. Biscuit and Molly require one walk a day as opposed to two, and they love to sleep when they are in the house. Biscuit likes to growl and threaten us when she doesn't want to do something, but she's fine. They dislike other dogs, however, so their walk must be timed at one in the afternoon with the hope of not running into any other dogs.

And so we have much more of our own time on this sit, but ironically no car. I must admit it's taken me a bit of time to get used to this house, though no fault of the house itself. The first night, I was leaning down into the fridge and came up quickly, smashing my head on the door and knocking one of the trays onto the floor, where it broke. Joe and I ordered the part online and are waiting for delivery. Then today I washed the bath rug and it changed color!

It's interesting to change residences. It's all about adaptability, patience, and being kind to yourself and each other in the process. Last night I spent two hours ordering groceries online only to find out that I couldn't use an American credit card for delivery.

The place itself is very comfortable and well-fitted with everything we need, including a bread machine. There's even an egg man right next door, so even if the grocery store is a mile and a quarter away, we can always make bread and have eggs! And this home has HDTV, and the entire Harry Potter series on DVD, so what more could you ask for?

The dogs are snoring on the couches while we watch a movie. My next challenge involves finding us the perfect sit for the first two weeks in March, which we have open right now. Today I wrote to a couple who live in the Lake District, though their dates are not defined. Fingers crossed that the perfect sit will work out—as they always do, as everything always does.

JANUARY 4

In this moment

I guess it's obvious that I am a pretty upbeat person. I can get knocked down by dogs or life, feel happy rain or shine, and generally, along with my partnership with Joe and with Reiki, continue to have a glass half full attitude towards life. But, for some reason unknown to me at this time, on a soul level I have landed with a thump in our second housesit in Greenfield.

I know, deep within, that this is an auspicious New Year, and one in which greatness will be discovered, provided I can get my own head out from under the covers long enough. Lately I've seen some not-so-nice sides of myself and have had to look hard at how I am living in each moment, what I eat, where my thoughts go, what makes me angry, what am I holding onto. Right now I don't feel as though light and joy and love are one with me all the time. I feel as though I am seeking them out, searching for them, but not always finding them.

People who know me might not recognize the shadow side of me. I almost do not recognize her myself, because I haven't seen her for a while. And I'm not exactly crazy about her sudden arrival in the midst of an altogether magical journey. But I asked for this on some level, when I asked to see the inside of me, to know myself better, to dig deeper into life, to be enlightened, please.

I've always been the good girl, ever since I was young and things were flying out of control at home. I was raised in a tender, beautiful, albeit dysfunctional family. Within our family circle, we experienced mental illness and drug and alcohol abuse along with devout Catholicism and lots and lots of love and goodness. All throughout my childhood, I somehow became the one they didn't worry about. And I guess in many ways I've carried that role over the course of my life. Perhaps it's time for this good girl to just be a girl, or rather a woman, in all her shining, glorious imperfections and while I am at it, to regard the present moment as just what it is—not to struggle, not to rage, not to try and change it into the reality that I think I want. This is what I have created, and if it is less than perfect then so what. Where are my thoughts? What am I going to create next?

Right now, today, in this moment, I feel sad, depressed, unhappy, homesick and missing my family, uncertain and unknowing in a strange place and yet, can I just be with it? Feel the feelings? Love the Self and the Other and know that they are one?

I know I shall emerge better, more knowing, gaining a deeper understanding of it all, a deeper sense of myself at large in the world if I can just *be* and live in the present moment.

This morning in bed I was praying for all those I want to share Reiki's love with. Here I've used the word prayer to describe sharing Reiki and if this is a way that makes more sense to you then so be it. For me, praying to my God and sending Reiki are inseparable. When I send Reiki to others via the frequency known as Reiki, or Universal Life Force Energy (much better and faster than the worldwide web), a channel to the Divine is opened in me at the same time. Flipping that around, when I open to the Divine energy, Reiki automatically flows through my hands and my heart. They are one and the same.

Normally sending Reiki puts me in a very serene place, but this time serenity was not where I was. My mind instead played its games of worrying about this or that. And then—just then—I asked myself, "Can I just be present? Can I just be in this moment, this very moment and very second that exist, without needing to make a grocery list of wants or worries?"

This time here is revealing me to myself and digging up the roots of the dead stuff within me that needs to be excavated. And what a ride it is. All my life I have been trying to escape ugliness, and perhaps the ugliness is me that I am trying to escape, aspects of myself that I have shoved deep within. Can I look at that and love it?

Here's to discovering the Light that is always alive and well within us all.

JANUARY 5

Our new sit

Several days have passed since I've visited this page and writing still seems to want to flow through me. There is much to say. Many conflicting emotions arose after hearing the news last night of Joe's elderly parents being moved yet again, this time to a nursing home. Though we knew it was coming, I still feel sadness for lives forever altered. It makes me realize how our choices affect others on such a deep level, and though it doesn't help to go into that train of thought, I ask myself, "What would have happened if… if we hadn't moved away to Colorado? Or we had come back East sooner? Would they be living with us now? And how would our lives be different? How would theirs?"

Joe isn't one for looking back. He feels he "earned" his freedom during all those years that he fulfilled his role as a dutiful son and nephew. And his freedom also meant my own, freedom to start a life in Colorado closer to our daughters, and to meet and guide and teach and love with Reiki as our guide. The choices we make.

All of the wonderful souls we've met out West and the astounding moments we have shared together have not been a life wasted or spent selfishly, but rather a life of service to others, a humble existence in many ways.

Yet one of my biggest challenges in life is a feeling of needing to be everywhere, taking care of everyone, much like a steward for the whole world—or at least the world as I know it. Perhaps this is why the Divine has brought me here to the UK, far away from everyone except Joe, so I can finally look inside myself and see what is there. As my Reiki friend Jen's Higher Self said to mine during a Reiki treatment she shared with me, "Live *your* life for you." When we allow Reiki to flow through us, we are often connected so deeply to our Higher Self that we receive intuitive messages for others from the Divine. That was the message she received for me. As is the way of things, Divine messages tend to come repeatedly until you listen. Shortly after, another dear friend of mine said to me, "Go. Discover. Enjoy yourself. You don't have to hold up the world." Two such messages I can no longer ignore. If we can all just live our lives to its fullest expression, standing on our own highest ground, what a world we can create.

JANUARY 6

She writes

Just signed on for a writing workshop webinar with one of the writing coaches I've worked with in Colorado named Alissa Johnson.[6] Alissa has helped me tremendously in ways that other writing coaches could not. She brings out the best in me by asking the right questions, coaxing me to tell the story about why I write or why I don't, who I am, what I want, and how can I get all that onto the page.

---

6 Alissa Johnson, www.writingstrides.com.

Looking back now at the beginnings of my writing journey, right before I published my first *Reiki News Magazine* article and before I met Alissa, I realize how far I have come in terms of how I look at myself and my own work, the way I come to the work, how much I value it (or am learning to do so). In some ways, this whole trip to the UK has been focused, at least for me, in terms of A: living at sea level for a while to see if I felt better, and B: creating an opening for writing. And lo and behold, not only do I feel better, but Joe does too! He told me yesterday that he feels so much more energy living out of the elevation that he can't believe it. And the opening for writing is simply based on the fact that we've stepped out of our lives, as it were.

This means that my pull to service has now shifted its focus to manifest itself through writing and finally, at long last, I am getting down to the page. Larry, my main writing audience at the moment, recently reminded me (yet another message) about "living my life," pointing out that life does in fact go so very quickly.

I am, though 58 (is that really right?), still of the eternal mind, the mind that thinks this fun lasts forever. But there is a knowing that things need to be said and need to be said now, that the words on the page are somehow more important now than they ever were before. And yet, at the same time, there is the observation that maybe I didn't write them before simply because I wasn't ready to. Now that I have finally arrived at the page, I recognize just how much I love this time.

JANUARY 8

Quiet days, full days

No matter what life brings, Reiki is always there for me, as is my loving Joe. Self-Reiki is a tremendous gift and one students are taught in their very first class. We try to impress on them the importance of simply giving Reiki to your own sweet self. It takes some effort to develop a practice of self-Reiki, for many of us find self-nurturing to be the most difficult practice of all. And when we feel low or life is not humming along, it can be even more so. Yet this is the time to dig in and do it.

So this morning, as I sat here in bed, giving myself morning Reiki and watching the daylight begin to show itself, I felt once more an excitement for the day to begin, to get out in it and explore. I took a walk with the pups alone, while Joe relaxed on the couch. Everything felt fresh, including me, as if I were experiencing the silence and wonder of nature for the very first time. Heaven was mine for a bit. I found a secret footpath to an enchanted pond, covered in a morning mist (I discovered later that this was part of Flitwick Moor). One of the things I love best in life is following new paths in the woods, uncertain of which way they will go. What a metaphor for my life.

The weather, though it looked damp and cloudy when I was inside earlier, turned out to be quite warm. In fact, I took off my scarf and hat and opened my coat after walking a while. The sun even peeked out when I was at the pond. I didn't want to go back to the house and wished I had a blanket and notepad and could sit and write there all afternoon, but dear Joe was waiting and the pups wanted to go home. Feeling blessed in so many ways, it *is* a privilege to be here on the planet today.

JANUARY 11

Finding an opening

As Joe and I walked this morning, we talked about the magic of our first sit in Colyton—the friendliness of the people, the sheer beauty of the landscape, the wonder of the ocean. We talked about how much we liked the pub there; it was a friendly place with great people and we seemed to fit right in like natives. We recognize we have yet to find a pub here that resonates with us like Kingfisher did in Colyton. We both realize that we are still deeply reliving our time in Colyton, yet we remain open because there is much more adventure ahead.

I took Joe to the little pond I found the day before and there we got kissed by the sun again! Then, with the magic that is the Universe, we met up with our next-door neighbors, Leo and Esme, on our walk home. We stood on the street for 15 minutes talking to them and ended up making a date to meet them at the pub at 4. They also told us about a nice little pub in Flitton called the Jolly Coopers that serves good, traditional English food. It will be about a half-hour walk, I imagine, so when we get a good day for it, we will walk there for lunch or dinner.

We've been looking at the menus of all the restaurants our homeowners recommended, and most of them are a cab ride away and look expensive. Joe and I are on a travel budget, which means that we do spend more money on certain things than we would at home but not however much we want. So hearty, traditional pub food is right up our alley on all counts!

Esme knocked on the door at four o'clock. It had just stopped hailing and was now just drizzling. Esme and Leo and Joe and I walked and talked our way to The Compasses and sat there for an hour or so, meeting up with their other friends. I felt very comfortable with all of them right away.

Later on our walk home, I commented to Joe about our most recent life lesson that evening. Just about the time I had begun to forget about being grateful for what is, instead of comparing it to what was, such as comparing this sit to the one before it, life reminded us both that there are always possibilities.

After talking to his mom for a long time last night, Joe at last went to bed. I stayed up and checked my emails, finding one from Harriet, our homeowner in Scotland, our last house-sit, who said she is going to let us drive her car—a Mini Cooper! We feel so amazed and blessed at the generosity of these people. Yippee! We will be able to get to the train station to go to Edinburgh and other local attractions. Harriet said most things are within 10 miles. And Joe wants me to drive this time. I think this may be our best sit yet! We will have just two cats—so our walks will be only if and when we want to go—which will probably be every day anyhow—a car, and we will be in Scotland!

We may also have a short holiday somewhere, not sure where yet, before we go to Scotland. More of the great unknown.

JANUARY 13

Tell me how you really feel

You know when you take on a housesitting assignment that you will, in fact, be getting a "free" place to stay. Don't misunderstand. This is an actual job. One aspect of your job is to take care of someone else's house, where you don't know how things work, which is why sometimes you knock the shelf off the refrigerator the first night you arrive and have to pay $40 to buy a replacement. Lesson Number One: Try not to be a klutz. Lesson Number Two: Mind your head and take your time.

Taking care of someone's home can involve many things, from cleaning to picking up mail to watering plants to mowing the grass (just not in January in England). But the main and most important part of your stay at people's houses involves taking care of their precious animals. Easy, right? I mean, I adore being with animals. But taking care of other people's animals is never quite like you expect it to be. Like the two lovable labs you can't wait to meet and you somehow have this vision of the lab you owned—a dear, sweet, fun girl you spent many hours roaming the fields with.

Instead, you might meet a male lab with a tendency to bark his head off every time anything or anyone goes by the house (which is quite frequently, owing that the house is right on the road), and a female who claims to know nothing about a leash and less about how humans might acquire a dislocated shoulder from her constant pulling.

I say this with tongue in cheek as I do miss them terribly now that we are no longer with them. We quickly grew to love their quirky but endearing ways: one diving under water like a duck going after minnows and the other running, always running with abandon and never learning the meaning of fetch, but always in the game somehow. I miss the long walks with them on the village paths and meeting folks from the town with their dogs. I have to say that I don't miss being dragged to the ground, although I learned a valuable lesson that day. I am *not* too old to fall really hard! Maybe I should take up horseback riding again. My bones must be pretty good!

The array of personalities one meets in caring for different animals makes the job unendingly interesting. There are the whiners, one of whom we are living with now. One of these girls has a set of lungs that suggest she'd like to try out for "The Voice," except she can't carry a tune. She whines to come inside, to come into our room when we are trying to still be asleep at 5:30 a.m. (even after letting her outside). But taking a page from Anna Twinney's book, I remind myself, through half closed eyelids, she's just communicating in the way she knows, and the solution comes when we cover up the chair and let her sleep in the bedroom with us in the mornings!

Whining (with the important addition of growling in various octaves) is *also* used when she *doesn't* want to do something—like go to the kitchen so you can pen her up and go out for a while—or when you try to wash the mud off her legs in the garage so you can let her into the house sooner. (Just trying to help.) And the funny thing is that when she is not growling or whining, she is endearingly pushing herself so close against you on the couch, you would think you were her personal heating system. It's sweet but does in fact make it a bit challenging to type when she is at your elbow. Lesson Number Three: It is said that all things outside of us are a mere reflection of what's inside. Maybe I should stop whining so much!

You also learn what it's like to live without a car, and therefore learn to be ever so grateful for the things you normally take for granted. Being without a car has its advantages, though, like building stronger leg muscles, and saving money for your next great and grand adventure in Edinburgh, where you and your darling husband will walk about and eat whenever you like and maybe buy a few cute gifts, and forget for three days that you are on a travel budget.

Being without a car also means you might meet neighbors like Leo and Esme, who kindly offer you both the use of their car (even though you won't borrow it) or their bikes, and you realize just how lovely people can be.

And there are ways to compensate for the lack of a car that also end up giving you a sunnier outlook (sunnier on the inside, you understand, because outside it may still be cloudy or raining). You can pay 20 quid for the taxi man to take you to the farm shop when neither you nor the driver has any idea where the shop is, while the meter keeps ticking away! But in the end he only charges you 10 quid—10 quid there and 10 quid back, that is. A bit pricey to buy a few sausages and a couple of bottles of beer, but there is the adventure factor.

Another thing you learn while housesitting is that not all beds are the same, which makes you ever so grateful for what you have. So when sleep does come, fully and without interruption from scratchy, whiny noises, it is pure bliss. And gratitude is really the driving force behind this trip: finding gratitude in a strange land; taking yourself out of your comfort zone and exploring what that feels like. Can you begin again, and again? Can you learn and change?

This is something I've always strived for—to continually test my adaptability in life. I truly believe it's what makes one able to find peace in any situation. Things you learn when you're in another country for several months include learning to really see yourself, and I mean see all of yourself: the good, the bad, and the downright ugly. You see your weaknesses and your flaws. You see your beauty and your peace (or lack thereof). You see your habits and you re-examine your place on the planet. You grow. You grow taller in your shadow. And it's only January.

JANUARY 14

In the words of Liz Gilbert

Last night, we watched *Eat, Pray, Love,* a favorite movie of mine adapted from the book of the same name written by my favorite author Liz Gilbert. There's a series of lines from the movie that I love. "In the end, I've come to believe in something I call the physics of the quest—a force in nature governed by laws as real as the laws of gravity. The rules of quest physics goes something like this: If you are brave enough to leave behind everything familiar and comforting, which can be anything from your house to bitter old resentments, and set out on a truth-seeking journey, either externally or internally, and if you are truly willing to regard everything that happens to you on that journey as a clue and if you accept everyone you meet along the way as a teacher and if you are prepared most of all to face and forgive some very difficult realities about yourself, then the truth will *not* be withheld from you."[7]

And I realized that although I am not in an ashram or working with a medicine man and I am not alone without my beloved, as the character Liz was, I am, both internally and externally, on a truth-seeking journey, the quest of physics that Liz speaks of. I am open to finding the truth of myself on this journey.

What if we lived our whole lives this way, being brave enough to continually go on a truth-seeking journey? We would live in a state of openness and receptiveness, following all the clues given to us, listening to our instincts and not being afraid to see and if necessary forgive the truth of ourselves. We would make magic and life would change all around us.

The other night when I couldn't sleep and got up to write stories about some of the people in my life, suddenly I was handed a beautiful truth about myself. For a moment, there in the living room of someone else's home, in the middle of the night, as I wrote about a great lifetime friend I have, I saw what she sees when she looks at me. I saw myself from the outside in. And it was wondrous, although it didn't last long, this exquisite feeling. In that moment, though, I felt a love for my own Self that went beyond anything I'd ever experienced in just that way.

For all seekers, I write this and humbly share. In love of truth.

---

7 Quote transcribed by this author from the movie, Eat, Pray, Love.

JANUARY 15

Becoming a family

Working with these very different types of dogs takes me back to my days of training horses. Dogs are not that much different. I have always found it to be an interesting challenge to see if dogs and humans will adapt to each other. Biscuit, our whiny growler of this sit, is actually turning a corner with us, and we are having fun getting to know our new animal friends. Molly is a sweet little thing and when we go for a walk she will wait all day long for you to throw a rock for her so she can chase it.

We were told that Biscuit and Molly might be a little bit better about meeting up with other dogs since their ring leader, Poppy, had been farmed out to the daughter's house. Joe and I at first were extremely cautious, knowing about their particular quirks, and took the prescribed walk at 1 p.m to the same field each day. But after a week of rain, that route became entirely too deep in mud, so I suggested a less muddy route that led to a beautiful loop past a quiet pond and a horse field.

We happily traced this loop each day, rarely running into other dogs. All was well until it rained about nine more times. Then the drying off process started to take forever. Yesterday I asked Joe if he was game to walk the dogs in town, in order to stay out of the deep mud, and so we did, up a hill past the elementary school and into an open field, which, on a scale of muddiness, didn't come close to the fields we'd been slogging through. The pups were ecstatic, as I believe their homeowners take them on the same walk every day. Biscuit, the one who typically reacts the most to other dogs, wasn't too bothered as she had her nose planted to the ground, happily smelling new territory. When we let her loose in the field she just ran.

Today was even more exciting for Biscuit as we walked the moors closer to the house. Once we unclipped her leash, she ran as if she hadn't been that free in a long while. Molly has gotten so much better that she doesn't even bark when she sees another dog.

Just like with Tigger and Roo in Colyton, we were brought together for a reason. With patience, love, and Reiki, we will continue to work together to form a human-canine pack that is in sync.

JANUARY 21

Day out!

This wonderful house is still playing tricks on me, as it did the first night when I crashed my head into the refrigerator shelf. Since then, I've unwittingly dyed the beige bath rug blue and broken the top of the butter dish. Based on this, we decided that a day out to do some shopping was in order.

Our trip to Bedford did us both good. We needed a spot of adventure. It was fun to walk through the woods past the mystical pond to Flitwick and hop on the train to Bedford. We are getting better at using the train ticket machine and all else. And so lovely to be going someplace on a train with no bags! We felt free. We got off the train at Bedford and found quite a large town with evidence of people with fewer economic advantages than in Greenfield. I started beaming Reiki out to everyone I saw on the street.

Beaming Reiki means to send Reiki over short distances. All it really takes is opening one's heart and setting an intention for the Reiki to flow to whomever wishes to receive it. We walked into the town center and found a thriving outdoor market. They were selling everything from veggies to scarfs to dead birds. The birds surprised me. There were a number of dead pheasants and partridges hung on a rack, still with their feathers on and everything.

The men shouted out from the stands as we walked past. "Get your bananas here!" or "Avocados: one quid!" I tried to buy one avocado but the man was selling a basket of them for a pound. I told him I just wanted one so he handed it to me no charge. Soft, but I didn't complain. How can you complain about a gift?

We wound through the town center to find Harpur, an indoor shopping center. The very first home shop we went into had a white butter dish and an off-white bath rug to act as replacements. They weren't exact but close enough, and quite reasonable at nine pounds, as both were on sale. Hopefully our homeowners will be happy. And it's not the end of the world; we're talking butter dish and bath mat here.

We found a really cozy cafe in Harpur that served nice sandwiches and soup for lunch, and we both had tea. Afterward we strolled through the market to the Ouse River. There was a gorgeous 18th century spa hotel called the Swan by the river—aptly named for there was a multitude of the biggest swans we had ever seen all along the river. I took so many photos of the swans that I think I will post an entire album of them. In Native

American medicine, swan means grace. We walked back through the market, and I took a picture of the pheasants and partridges that were hanging up for sale. A bit grotesque, but the feathers fascinated me, and how often do you see something like that in the US?

We returned to the train, which we caught immediately. Twelve minutes later we were back in Flitwick, walking the one-and-a-half miles with our two bags of goodies. Leg weary, we arrived home and took most of the night to give rubs or Reiki to our sore parts. Joe rubbed my back; I gave him Reiki on his knee. It is wonderful to have a partner that can do not only massage but also Reiki. We take care of each other. A great and good day it has been. And just so grateful that we are able to walk so far and be so active.

JANUARY 25

Right mind

I am reading a mind-opening book called *The Inner Heart of Reiki: Rediscovering the True Self*[8] by Frans Stiene, and it's quite unlike anything that I've ever come across before. Perhaps the student is ready so the teacher has appeared.

I've even got Joe interested in reading it, and he doesn't read many books. He has it on his iPad and I on my laptop so we are reading it at

---

8 Frans Stiene, The Inner Heart of Reiki, Rediscovering Your True Self, (Winchester, UK: Ayni Books, 2015). Kindle edition.

almost the same time. There is an increased Reiki energy in the house since he has started to read it, and my comprehension and interest in the book has deepened in the past two days. I bought it a while ago, read the first 10 pages, was blown away, recommended it immediately to a couple of students, and then stopped reading it altogether. But now I am buzzing through happily.

In Reiki we are taught special symbols. These symbols are empowered by Reiki and are used for different healing intentions, such as mental and emotional healing, focus and power, or for offering distance healing.

The configurations of the symbols, along with the names of some of them, originally were intended to be held sacred, close to one's heart, and not shared except in a Reiki class. This practice is still honored by many Reiki practitioners, even though the symbols appear all over the Internet. Stiene explains in his book that the names of certain symbols are considered to be kotodama, meaning that the name itself contains the soul of the word. It is believed that keeping the name sacred as well as the symbol helps to retain its power.

In the book, Stiene explains the meaning of the first symbol in Reiki, commonly known as the Power symbol, as meaning "to have Right Mind."[9] When I first read those words I was in anything but Right Mind. My mind has been a muddle lately, going back and forth and up and down and sideways all the time, about everything great and small. I have not been able to make any decisions whatsoever, and I have felt very much like the mouse on the proverbial wheel.

---

9 Stiene, The Inner Heart.

One of the exercises Stiene gives the reader is to chant the Reiki symbols over and over and over—hundreds, even thousands of times—in order to absorb the blessings, the intent they have for us. Earlier today, I chanted the name, or kotodama, of the first symbol, for several minutes, and I began to feel lighter. I felt this fuzzy cloud that had been hanging over me lifting and underneath was something vaguely familiar that I recognized as me.

Later this afternoon, I found myself joking with Joe with a lightheartedness that I haven't felt for days. And tonight after dinner, as I cleared the table and focused on the moment in front of me, blissfully, I felt my Right Mind enter the room just as if she'd been there all along, which of course she had.

I do believe part of the healing journey is also in recognizing the discord within me, surrounding it in love, and then gently sending it on its way. Using the mantra of the Reiki symbol allowed Reiki to complete the healing and raise my vibration once more.

Or, as Stiene puts it, to "take off another lampshade and shine a bit more brightly."[10]

At last the time is drawing near for our next adventure. It's been a time of rebirth in many ways for me. I didn't realize the significance of it until we were here for a while, but it's becoming clearer each day.

---

10 Stiene, The Inner Heart.

We've become pretty friendly with Leo and Esme by now, and we found a note at the front door this morning asking us out to dinner tonight. We went to a place called Blackbirds in Flitwick, and it was lovely to be driven somewhere after being on foot for a month. We had a really fun time at Blackbirds. What a well-priced meal! For example, a burger with chips and side greens was £4.49 and for £1 extra you could get a pint. They invited us in for a coffee at their cozy cottage on our return, and we happily said yes.

Esme wants us to keep in touch, so we've become Facebook friends, and we talked about getting together when we come back this way in early March for our sit in Huntingdon, which is near Cambridge and just an hour from here. Esme said that they will come over, and we can go out for a meal.

And so, all of our plans are now set. We've found a wonderful house and pet-sit in Huntingdon, and then comes our three-day holiday in Edinburgh. We will take the train there and then take it back down to our last sit in the Scottish Borders in a town called St. Boswell. It will be exciting to spend time with the Scots and see the differences and hear how English is spoken there.

We have found the English to be lovely people. Traditional, perhaps, but they have a lot of class when it comes to knowing how to treat people and be hospitable. I told Esme tonight, "You both have been so great to us," and she just looked at me and said, "Well, that's what ya do!"

New places are wonderful, new walks magical, but connecting with people and animals—that is what life is all about.

JANUARY 27

Who is my God?

    This morning, in a quiet moment, two thoughts arose that led me to that question. The first one was: I need to have time with my God. And the one that followed was: And why can't I have my God exactly the way I see her, experience her just for me when I do, love her with the specialness that such a relationship can bring?

    As I took some time and began to explore those thoughts, I suddenly came to the realization that I've missed my alone time for the past few years. Though great years they've been with Joe, who has retired, our lives have been spent pretty much together mostly all the time every day. And I, being of a nature that wants to be companionable and pleasing, tend to put my own needs last and go along with what pleases others until there's no time in the day left for me—a very common and sometimes, but not always noble feminine trait.

    However, I guess I thought that wanting time alone was somehow a privilege that I had to earn. Today, I see that it is a serious matter of a lack of self-love and of learning to prioritize yourself, accepting that your gifts do matter enough to make them important.

    And here is another aspect of seeing the inside of me—realizing that if I serve others too much and myself not enough, where is the balance? The real aha moment came when I realized that what I get out of being alone is simply time with my God to see more of myself, just as I do when

I spend time with nature, time with quiet, time with my thoughts if I want to go there, time to create, or just time to let go. Spending time with my God or the God within me is a greater service to the world than anything else I can do on this day or any day.

JANUARY 28

New day, new deal

Today we left Jacob and Jill's house in Greenfield. They were so nice when they saw us and just laughed about the bath rug and the broken butter dish. Jill said I didn't have to buy a new one. Really nice folks. They were very excited about their trip to South Africa, and we had some interesting conversation about the Nelson Mandela Museum they visited, which led into a discussion of apartheid.

We took little Biscuit and Molly for one last walk around the block while their recently returned owners showered and got settled, as our train didn't leave until 10:50 a.m. and there was still plenty of time (or so we thought). When we returned from our walk, the six of us (four humans and two dogs) sat around talking away again, this time about Harry Potter. Jacob and Jill were huge fans, as evidenced by their collection of movies and books on the subject. They liked that we watched the whole series while staying there. The dogs were funny because they sat on the couch with Joe and me while the four of us talked instead of sitting on their owners' laps. I guess they were sensing our departure. Jill and Jacob were pleased at how happy they seemed, and we told them what a comfortable stay we'd had.

The time got away from us all and we ended up leaving late and had a very quick ride to Bletchley. We made the train with about two minutes to spare. The ensuing rush left Joe feeling a bit unsettled, and the time to get off came quickly. I stood up and asked Joe to start getting the bags down to depart, and I think his mind was still unsettled from the initial rush of getting on the train in the first place.

At any rate, he got off the train without his iPad. We didn't realize it right away as Nikki picked us up with a sick baby, and the day rolled on in the manner that it does when with Nikki and baby—fast and furious. It wasn't until hours later that Joe asked Nikki about his little black bag, and we all gave a search to find that it was indeed missing. Nikki rang the train station, saying that lots of people hand things in when they get left on the train. Joe was very upset over it and kicking himself in the arse. (If you could physically do that, I'm sure he would have.)

I do understand; if it were my laptop I'd be crushed. But we all reassured him that it would turn up.

Nikki is still juggling many balls in the air, namely PhD work, teaching online courses, having an injured back from the car accident she had when we were there at New Year's, and taking care of darling Henry (a full-time job in itself), who has had more than his share of illnesses in the first nine months of his life. He has been feeling poorly with the flu just now. His eyes were glassy and his usual smile not present, although he perked up for a bit when we got home. But later, after sleeping on Nikki's lap for an hour or two, he woke up burning hot. She took his temp and it was the equivalent of 102.7. We both thought she should ring the doctor.

In response to her call, the doctor arranged to see them in just ten minutes, at which time he confirmed that it was nothing more serious than the flu, but to give Henry meds more often and call him if his temperature goes higher than 4.0° C. I believe that would be about 104° F. Home we went, where Joe crashed out by 8 p.m., as did Nikki and Henry. Mom and baby hadn't gotten a wink of sleep the night before.

That left Al and me the only ones still conscious. I've never talked a lot to Alex although I like him very much. He is quite funny but talks very fast and I sometimes get nervous around him because I'm afraid I won't understand him. But tonight was different somehow as I suddenly just saw him very clearly and I liked what I saw—a truly gentle person who is eager to please. I decided to devote myself to really listening, instead of being nervous. He made us each a small, frozen pizza and we enjoyed them with a couple of beers in front of the telly, and he talked a lot to me, more than he ever has before.

He told me stories of all the places he's traveled, as a boy and then as a man, and we spoke of religion and reading and technology. Soon I was longing for sleep and so I bid him goodnight.

Traveling teaches you in many ways, whether it is about finding the beauty that exists in everyone if you look closely enough or learning to be at peace with yourself in uncomfortable situations. I am reminded once more of *Eat, Pray, Love* in which the medicine man tells Liz, " Keep your feet grounded so firmly on the earth that it's like you have four legs. Stop looking at the world through your head. Look through your heart, instead.

That way you will know God."[11]

JANUARY 29

A different day altogether

Though I guess one could say that yesterday had its challenges, today was totally different and yet challenging in its own way too. The challenge took a slight shift from Joe to me this time. He woke up after his long sleep with a "knowing" that some kind person would have turned in his iPad.

But first there was sweet Henry, still sick as can be but a bit brighter. I sat with him in the morning, and he fell asleep in my arms. Nikki then had a chance to take care of the ponies and try to sort out some coursework until her desktop crashed. They have two horses, Molly and Summer, and one pony named Ginger, along with many sheep.

Nikki and I switched places. I gave a sleeping Henry to her and sat at my laptop with phone-in-hand to simultaneously call the train station's lost and found department and fill out an online form for "left luggage." Neither achieved any measure of satisfaction for an hour or so until I fooled the buttons on the automated system and finally spoke to a live person at the Birmingham New Street Train Station Left Luggage Department (don't know who you call for the Right Luggage Department!).

His name was Adam and I think he was wearing wings. He became my

---

[11] Elizabeth Gilbert, Eat, Pray, Love (New York: Riverhead Books, 2007). Kindle edition.

new guardian angel when he announced that yes, he had one such small black bag with an iPad in it along with a toothbrush, razor, and Sudoku book! All we had to do was get on another train to Birmingham and pay 20 quid to pick it up. Easy. Except when I went to book the train ticket, my debit card was turned down, leaving me with a question that threatened to challenge my peaceful state for the next three hours whilst I pondered if anyone had gotten our bank numbers.

It's easy to become paranoid whilst overseas and using strange ATM machines. But I put it firmly to the back of my mind, reminding myself of two of our Reiki slogans: "Everything is already alright" or "Everything is already being taken care of." Joe's iPad being kindly returned proved that unequivocally.

We booked the tickets using Nikki's card and were on our way. Birmingham New Street Station had just undergone a major facelift and it was beautiful with posh little eating places and a nice chocolate shop! We arrived at Lost Luggage to pick up the iPad, and the young men there laughed with us, joking about America. I showed them the picture of my car buried in the snow back in Pennsylvania. They said they hadn't seen snow that deep since they were young boys. One of the men asked Joe if he wanted him to tape the iPad to his body (after Joe joked about it), and we carried on.

I felt we needed a treat to celebrate, so we stopped quickly at one of the sandwich shops and had a bite. The food was good even though we paid train station prices. But that's what you do when you travel. Next, we popped into the chocolate shop and bought a few treats for Nikki and Al then dashed to catch the train and away we went once more–the wonder of travel.

Nikki and a smiling Henry were there to greet us at the train station, and after coming home to their little slice of paradise, I contacted the bank in Colorado to sort out the debit card issue (all good), and in doing so, made a new friend when the bank employee asked for my Facebook info so she could look at our pictures of England! I also booked train tickets over the phone with my credit card for our short holiday in Edinburgh.

It turns out there will be a six-nation rugby match there that weekend, and our B&B hosts said the place would be full of French militants, as the Scots are playing the French. Al came home from work, and we all settled in for a nice evening of talking and watching a little telly (Al loves his telly) and again eating pizza.

These two people and their son are so dear to my heart, and this time with them is so very precious. It makes me happy to be here and be able to help Nikki in small ways, like cleaning up the kitchen or feeding the ponies or watching Hen. It means a lot to us both, and I have a beautiful connection with Henry. He and I get on like two peas in an English pod.

Tomorrow.... Grasscroft! Nikki was researching it last night and said it is a very expensive area. Grasscroft is one of the Saddleworth villages in the borough of Oldham, just outside the city of Manchester. Liverpool is also nearby, home of the Beatles. I'd love to go to Liverpool or maybe see a show in Manchester. And do a lot of writing and yoga and walking! I love life and my enthusiasm for it.

February in Uppermill

JANUARY 30

What I'm learning in the UK

We've been here just two months now, to the day. When leaving Nikki's little abode this morning (crazy Al drove us to the bus station—always an adventure), she said, "Think of all the things you've learned and all the different parts of the country you've seen and have yet to see. You've seen more of England than I have!"

So now we are on to a new part of the country. Nikki said it would look completely different, and I am feeling very excited. We left Alex with happy goodbyes and got on the bus to Manchester.

It turned out that the bus was so very crowded that Joe and I could not sit together. Manchester is large, over half a million people, so it makes sense that a lot of people would be going there. The woman just in front of me was talking loudly on her cell phone so I'm glad I remembered my ear plugs! First time I've used them like this; makes me feel like a real traveler.

I was listening to "Music to Journal By" by Julie True while I wrote on the bus. I use her music a lot when I teach Reiki, and I love it for that. This was only the second time I'd used it to write, however, and it worked well here; it put me in another space, far away from a crowded bus and yet at the same time closer to the people on it.

What I've learned so far in England goes something like this:

Number One Rule. Always endeavor to stay dry. Wear a waterproof jacket with a hat or a hood.

Always wear Wellies unless you are going to be street walking (in the non-professional sense:).

When arriving in a new town, first find out where the best locals' pub is (and if you can walk to it; very important) and then where the grocery store is.

When you buy a train ticket, take along the card that says that you purchased the ticket along with the BOOKING REF number to the station when you pick up the tickets! Otherwise the machine won't give them to you.

If you don't pre-purchase your ticket and for some reason, you can't buy a ticket at the train station, you can always get on the train anyway. The train crew will let you pay, so you won't end up in jail.

If you leave something on the train, don't weep. Call the number for Left Luggage and pretend it's been over 72 hours and just keep pushing buttons until you get a real person at the train's final destination station office.

If you're going to take the train a lot while you travel, plan ahead and buy a Railcard. It will save you lots of money (a third off all tickets).

Keep searching for lower fares and you will find them. Sometimes you might have to buy two tickets to get where you are going and you can save a lot of money that way. For instance, from Edinburgh to Northampton you might get a ticket to London and then another to Northampton.

If you figure out the best way to exchange money and not pay fees please write and let me know.

Men order full pints in the pub while women order half.

People like to keep fresh flowers in their front windows.

Everyone walks, even when they are nearly 100.

Despite what Alex says, most Brits seem to like Americans. At least they liked *us,* or else they were good at faking it. If you aren't really loud and you don't talk fast, most people will think you're Canadian anyway.

Be prepared to see a whole lot of green and not have to use moisturizer as much.

Get an international phone plan or a SIM Card pay-as-you-go phone. It helps to have a phone.

Have a phone card or ten for international calls. People at home want to hear from you, especially your Mom.

If you have a British friend like Al, get him to buy you an old junker for 100 quid before you get there and then let him sell it after and keep the profit (should have done, but didn't).

Above all, keep smiling—even on the gloomy days. The sun will come out again.

Keep a journal.

Get used to people apologizing for the weather.

Many bathrooms have very deep tubs. Yay! Remember your bubbles.

Buses (National Express) are much less expensive for most trips, but the train is ALWAYS much faster! Given the choice, try to take the train.

Send chocolate home, and be prepared to pay three times what you paid for the chocolate to ship it there.

It's raining again? Trust me, the sun will come out eventually, but when it does, make a run for it. Get outside quickly and savor the moment because it might not last.

Don't order anything called blanch bait unless you like eating bait!

Learn as much as you can as quickly as you can about how to get where you need to go.

Libraries are the BEST resource. You can get a library card in England even if you don't live there. You can check out books, use their computers, and print there as well (10p per copy). Also, they usually have bus schedules. I found that borrowing books and buying ebooks was the way to go when traveling. Though I prefer to have a real book (I like to read in the tub), an ebook is handy from time to time if there is something I want right away.

Remember there's always more to learn and that's the fun of it!

FEBRUARY 2

All in a day's move

We arrived in Manchester after a long bus ride, realizing that we didn't know what our house owners, Ava and Jack, looked like. It hadn't seemed as if it would matter since I, ever trusting, expected them to be there with open arms when we got off the bus (or at least carrying a sign saying "Welcome Joe and Rose").

After waiting a bit and trying to get the usually handy Whatsapp to work on my phone, I asked someone at the desk if I could call and leave a message, thinking I would confirm our station just in case. Little was I aware that the number I had in my phone was their home phone. But onward I moved doggedly, sitting down next to a friendly woman who reminded me a bit of my friend Norma. I told her my situation and asked if she would kindly send my new friend Ava a text to confirm where we were waiting, again not realizing we were calling a landline.

In the meantime, Ava was texting me (to no avail) to let me know they were at another station. But soon enough, Jack was there and taking us to meet Ava and drive home. The day, which had turned sunny, now turned to hail and snow on the way back to Saddleworth, where we would spend the next month in the village of Grasscroft. We could see the Pennines, a mountain range that separates Northwest England from Yorkshire, through the clouds and imagined just how beautiful they would be on a clear day. Nikki was right! We were in a very different part of England.

We met the chickens and the two well-loved cats, Sarafina and Mufasa. Beautiful cats they were, and they seemed to warm to us pretty quickly, which made Ava very pleased. She is a proud mama with her kitties, and it was very important to her that we give them a lot of love.

Their home felt very comfortable and boasted a wonderful view of the Pennines from their sliding glass doors in the living room that opened onto a small balcony. Joe and I were tired from the journey, but enjoyed the time with our hosts. They prepared a nice dinner of salmon and roasted vegetables with a mixed greens salad with feta cheese. The meal, cooked by Jack, was delicious, and we started to get to know them. They are both retired police officers. In fact, Jack just retired the day we arrived. We all turned in by 9 p.m.

The next day we shared a breakfast of porridge and tea, after which Ava announced she was going for a swim at the local gym. "I've just read that women should eat prior to exercise for maximum fat burning potential," she told me as we cleaned up the kitchen. Ava, a pretty slim redhead, obviously works at looking good and enjoys it. She is fun, intelligent, and interesting. I look forward to knowing her better.

She and Jack bought a home in South Africa after visiting a few times and realizing how inexpensive housing was there. Now they can go for long periods, especially since Jack has just retired. They told us about Cape Town and what the people are like, the food, the weather, the politics. It is at this point that I know without a doubt that I am in another country, because I don't have these kinds of conversations at home. We live in a small mountain community where many of the people have lived all their lives. While some do travel, more often it is in the US. Europeans are so aware of what is going on in other countries, while I think we in America are so focused on ourselves.

The next day Ava and Jack kindly took us shopping to Aldi, a big store with very good prices for food. I found it a bit disconcerting at first as they began to follow me down the aisle, which was packed with people. I recognized that they were being helpful, but I've never shopped with people watching me before. They soon figured it out and went on ahead. Jack and I agreed to split the cost of the fish for tonight's dinner with the word "deal," a word that threaded itself through our day.

In the car, Jack began to show us all the roads, how to get into town, and where the bus stop was. Joe and I sat in the back seat where the windows were all fogged over, and I tried to fight feeling overwhelmed, telling myself it would be fine. But what I was really thinking is that it seemed so very far to Uppermill, which is where the shops, restaurant, and train station were, and that I would never be able to find anything.

I realized that I was just tired and things would look better in the morning, which they did. The next day Ava and I went together to an appointment she had for a spray tan at her spa in Ashton. We rode in her two-seater Audi and it was such fun! Plus I could see much better and began to understand where everything was. She showed me a footpath that went down to the bus station and when Joe and I walked it later, we realized that it was really close, though we will no doubt build new muscles in our legs since the way back is very steeply uphill.

While Ava was engaged in her tanning appointment, I walked downstairs to the indoor market. There was everything one could want: fish, veggies and fruits, cheeses, meats, breads and sweets. The smell of fresh baked bread and coffee from the roastery down the aisle filled the air. The colors of the market—the white fish, the greens and reds and purples of the vegetable stand—it all sends a thrill through me and I want to be everyplace at once. Looking at it and shopping for it is almost as good as eating it. I decided to walk all the way around the square of the market center and then choose what to buy.

What I discovered was "you name it, they had it" and at very reasonable prices. I wandered around, taking it all in, and left with a bag of plums, chocolate-covered peanuts for my chocoholic hubby, and some fresh plaice fish (a type of flounder) for dinner that night. I'm happy and feel more like myself after a good night's rest and a new adventure.

Ava and I shared stories about our lives and loves and we commiserated over being redheads who aren't really red anymore (except with the help of our friends: hair dye and a good colorist). We lamented over the price of vanity, and she shared her secret shampoo, promising me that if I like it, she will mail it to me in the States if I mail her Coffeemate creamer (she loves to mix it in her porridge). Deal.

Later that day, I shared a Reiki session with Ava before she left. It was so wonderful to share it with someone new, especially here. I realized as I spoke to her about Reiki what a level of comfort I have gained in talking to new people about Reiki, about walking my talk. She totally loved it. It was one of those sessions when you can tell straightaway that the person receiving is really opening to it fully. In my perception, it has to do with how the energy draws immediately and there is an instant connection. There is always an energetic connection when giving someone Reiki, but it's always different, sometimes stronger than other times.

Then there are times when the connection is so electric and instant and you just know that the person is really receiving. You cannot have preconceived notions of it all, though, for the people you think in your mind will be the least accepting might be the ones who will blow you away. I feel grateful for the open and trusting nature I have always been lucky to have, for Reiki came to me without resistance. The first Reiki treatment I ever had was so relaxing that I fell sound asleep and missed most of it!

While treating Ava, my hands became fiery hot, and she too observed this, as well as a feeling of her body being split in two (I was mainly working on her left side, where she had a shoulder issue). She also felt a slight sensation of pressure, which I've found with many clients and find most interesting. There are so many things about Reiki that are interesting to me: How the energy works, why it works in different ways all the time, and how it can just "be" there at my fingertips at any time.

Ava and I were both on a Reiki high, and as they put the final touches on their packing, Joe and I went for a walk behind the house. We wanted to see just how far of a walk it was to Ava's favorite pub, The Old Original in Scouthead, a nearby village. The wind was whipping so hard my Tilley hat blew through the field until Joe captured it and put it in his pocket. Love those pockets. They carry everything for me.

We walked across the footpath that went straight through several open fields, one of which had a half-torn sign that said "bull in field." Before we stepped over the stone steps that led into it, we looked right and left for Mr. Bull but saw no sign of him. Halfway across, Joe grabbed me and said, "There's the bull!" And I giggled in response. That's Joe, his sense of humor always intact.

The going got rather mushy and even though we were wearing our Wellies, we decided to turn back. We sighted the pub in the distance, but it may best be a taxi ride in winter. It would make a lovely spring walk, perhaps.

I had at least seen the pub yesterday, when Ava and I were out driving, and it looked amazing—a genuine, old-fashioned pub with a view to die for. Even though Joe and I didn't make it all the way to the pub on our walk today, our reward was there when we turned back to walk to our temporary home. The view was widespread and absolutely stunning, the hills rolling like soft waves into one another, guiding your eyes to the Pennines in the distance. It was cold and windy but so very exhilarating that I felt I could spread my arms around nature and capture her in a big heart hug.

I love this land. We haven't seen anything like this since we've been in England. Ava told me that they call her street Millionaire's Row. I feel like a million, breathing easily here, walking in the wind over new land not knowing where it will lead. We got back to the house in time to say goodbye to our homeowners and felt excitement stirring within us about our new sit.

FEBRUARY 1

Looking for the inside of Me

While we continue to "do" many things in the outer world on this trip, and I continue to journal those things, many other things are happening to me in my inner world at the same time.

For example, I have decided to truly begin taking meditation seriously again. Oh, but those who know me may be shocked by this revelation. I am, after all, a Reiki teacher and yes, Reiki is a form of meditation, and I get very quiet when I practice Reiki or give a treatment or facilitate experiences in classes. And it's all quite good. But my regular meditation practice comes and goes—mostly goes these days.

And so I will begin again, as I continue to do. After two months of no yoga practice, I have begun to bring yoga into my early mornings followed by meditation to the inspiring sound of Julie True. I am starting small with just 20 minutes of meditation, but I know enough to know that is enough—for now—because it is what I can do. Even though I have read about it, talked about it and taken courses in it, there is no substitute for simply…doing it.

Another aspect of me that I want to stretch and reshape is my relationship with food and how to make wiser choices. Before our homeowners left, one the many things we discussed was dieting and Ava told us about the 5/2 diet, in which you take two days a week for fasting, eating only 500 calories on those two days and whatever you want on the other five. She said it transformed her body and that they both have been able to keep weight off for some time. I asked Joe if he would do it with me, and we made a plan to start the next day. Ava found a cookbook with recipes that include calories. Yes, my body desires to be lighter and also I'd like to develop more awareness of my eating habits and find a greater discipline within that.

So the things that I thought I was here to do keep falling away, while other things are unfolding in ways I never thought about. It is a time in my life right now for taking stock, for sitting still, for reflecting, for re-clarifying and re-inventing myself. Writing is a big part of that process, and words cannot convey the depth of my gratitude for being able devote myself to the practice of writing.

Today I got a book from the library (I am trying to get a library card in each county I visit) and the back showed that the author had published about 20 other books, all beautiful colors and interesting-looking stories.

And I envisioned for a moment that it was me. I could see how fulfilling it would be to publish all those books, and the knowing came to me that once I get my first book finished it will just continue to happen over and over. One creative thought will lead to the next and you won't be able to stop me if you try. At least that's what I see.

The day was cloudy and windy for most of the morning into afternoon. Joe was taking a nap when I looked out and saw the chickens were out and it looked like they were in the neighbor's yard. I called to Joe, and we both went outside, but they were okay; they just had pushed through a little door into a run that used to belong to them. Joe opened the shed to get them some corn and they cheerfully went back into "their" yard. Joe put a log behind the door so it wouldn't blow open or get pushed open again.

Around 2 o'clock, we saw the sun winking at us and decided to claim it. We started walking down to the Lovers Lane bus stop (our closest), and we both felt like continuing just a bit. So our first goal was to see how far it was to the Farrars Arms, the nearest pub. Being that it is literally all downhill toward Uppermill, we reached the pub easily and voiced our next goal of reaching the train station, just to see how far it was. Accomplished. So why not walk all the way into Uppermill village and show Joe around, since I'd been there the day before with Ava. We decided that we would catch the bus back to Lovers Lane.

The village of Uppermill is small, but filled with many interesting eating places, pubs, a butcher, a post office, a pharmacy, a small co-op, and more. I love the old feel of it and how you descend to it from Millionaire's Row. We made some friends in the post office where we bought another phone card (good to be well-stocked!) and everyone gave us helpful advice about where to go and what to see. Most of them suggested going into Manchester, as they have nice shops and great restaurants, but it's hard to explain to people that we truly want to experience the village life and the countryside.

After a few more quick stops, we crossed over to the bus, the 184, to go back to Lovers Lane. It came twice in 20 minutes, both times picking up schoolchildren only. The schedule read that another bus wasn't due until 7 p.m. (it was 4 something) so we decided to walk back home—uphill, mind you; perhaps this is why they call it Uppermill. The road we walked in on, though quite picturesque with massive stone walls on either side, giant stone homes on one side, and the canal below on the other, was noisy with traffic, so I suggested to Joe that we might try the trail along the canal. We weren't sure where it would take us but it led in the same general direction. This is me in my element—uncharted territory, seeing if I can find my way.

The walk along the canal provided such a quick and keen relief from the sound of the cars. We saw some boats dredging the canal along the way. After a bit we came to a bridge crossing in the direction of the road that we came in on, so we followed across it, and up a steep hill (they are all steep here). There was a beautiful footpath through the woods that took us to the next road, which led us to another footpath to the next road, which was ours. We were only a little ways now from Lovers Lane, where we turned onto another footpath and up another steep climb to the house. Whew!

I had to stop several times to catch my breath and Joe was in a sweat when we arrived home, both tired, but so happy for our time out. We did it! Now we know we can get to the bus stop, Farrars pub, and the train station. And we can walk into the village. We just have to sort out the bus to come back or catch a taxi. That puzzle will be solved another day.

Tired and very hungry by this time (Day One of our 500 calorie fast), I made our simple meal of plaice fish and salad, which tasted wonderful. We watched a fun movie, and Joe went to sleep early while I settled into the upstairs room, which is next to our bedroom, now designated to be my yoga/meditation cave, and did some journaling. I call it a cave because the ceilings are sloped like an attic and there's only one window that looks out onto the chickens by day and the stars by night. Mufasa and Sarafina are happy, the chickens are in their coop for the night, and I continue on my journey to find the inside of me.

FEBRUARY 3

A month of writing

This month must be one of resolutions. Okay, so it's a month into the new year, but who's counting? I've decided to dedicate this month to refining the lessons I have begun to learn here about myself.

I've started my writing course this week and so far it is a blast. We are given a writing prompt each day, and the story that came through with the prompt today still has me feeling very curious about writing fiction. It feels as though I have many words that have been building up inside of me for all of these years, now shouting to get out. I don't know if other writers feel this way or not, but I continue to move writing forward in importance, and I am loving every minute of it so far. In fact, the more I choose to sit and write for the pure pleasure of it instead of feeling as though I *should* write today, the more exhilarating it becomes. It is like my own secret gift that I can give to myself, a time to be with me. Joe said tonight, "Think of the other people you can make happy through your writing," but I can't fathom that part yet. All I know is that I don't believe you have to feel pain to be a writer; indeed, it should be a thing of joy, that of creating.

Today we saw blue sky after a sketchy morning, and Joe and I walked all the way across the open fields, the sun at our backs, to the Old Original pub. It was quite a walk but the reward came when walking mostly downhill on the return and facing straight into the glorious sunshine. What more can you ask for? A day of true contentment and simplicity, we came back home, gave the chickens some corn, had a bite to eat, and settled onto the couches to rest and watch an afternoon movie, the sun streaming in through the wall of windows that faces the Pennines. We both took turns napping, and I realized that this is one luxury I never afford myself—to fall asleep for a little while after a long walk in the cold air. What a great idea! I think we should both do it more often. One of the things the 5/2 diet recommends is more sleep.

And speaking of treating ourselves gently and well, we have both booked in for an Indian head massage next week. A young woman named Linzie is coming here to our temporary home to do it, and the fee is only 25 quid for an hour! What a find. We are both very much looking forward to it. I truly appreciate the blessings in this life. I know there are some who live on a grander scale—for example, our homeowners. They sent a text saying they had just boarded a luxury train on the way to their South African home and enjoyed a four-course meal on the train.

And while I am very happy for them and know they both worked very hard to earn these luxuries, I don't feel envious even a tiny bit. I feel a fullness of blessings just for the luxury of a tub to soak in and a good meal. To have a wonderful massage is, frankly, over the top. And to stay in such a lovely place with a contented cat sleeping next to you is life complete.

Tonight we took a taxi to the Old Original and had a dinner out. It was very good. Joe had pulled pork in a taco bowl with chips, and I a small salad with cheese and onion pie. After fasting yesterday I found myself full before I finished even a third and was surprised that my attitude towards food had changed a bit even after one day. Not to say I didn't truly enjoy eating, but my attachment to the food itself seemed different. Maybe that's the whole point. Tomorrow is our second day this week of the fast. Here's to transformation.

FEBRUARY 4

To see my soul light shine

In meditation this morning, I waited for a prayer, an affirmation for this day. What does my soul desire today? And what came was this: that I wish to see my Soul Self the way others see me. Perhaps that is the quest of this journey—to shine a Light so bright that it reflects back at me at every turn.

This brings to mind the story of my friend Mary.

Her name was Mary K (and she didn't sell cosmetics). Instead, she came to me as a real-life good fairy, but made of flesh and bones. Fun and funny, beautiful and ever so kind. Mary K and I met when I was in massage therapy school. This came after my great escape from Texas (surely we all have at least one of those!). I knew there were many parts of me that needed healing, and I chose to experience my own healing through learning to heal others. I went all in and signed up for massage therapy school at age 50.

I remember the first night we were in class, introducing ourselves to the group. Mary spoke softly but clearly and told us she was a mother of two boys and some other details I can't remember now, but at the end she said simply, "I am a Reiki Level I Practitioner." I had received a Reiki treatment once, and I knew enough to know that I was interested in learning more. I was surprised that suddenly there was this woman talking about Reiki. But there are no coincidences and Reiki calls you when it does.

We started our program of learning massage in July 2007 and for several months Mary and I talked about Reiki, in between all the other things we found to talk about. She became my sounding board, my intuitive. She brought forth her wisdom like fresh flowers on the wounded earth of my heart. I'd been kicked around and knocked down, and felt as though my bruises showed, yet Mary saw the beauty in me. Even in my half-resurrected state, she saw my soul light shine. There wasn't anything I couldn't do in Mary's eyes. We became, as Forrest says, like peas and carrots at school. Wherever you saw Mary, you saw me.

I remember one night in particular when she and I were giving massages side by side in the classroom. The lights were dim, and I was gently massaging my fellow student's head, my eyes closed. Mary leaned over to me and said, "Rose, you should learn Reiki. You are already doing it anyway."

In January 2008, she took me to a reading given by her friend and Reiki Master teacher, Cristina, who gave us all a private reading, and it was shortly after that I decided to sign up for a Level I Reiki class, despite not having the money for the class. At that time, I had a very "broke" mentality; after borrowing $10 grand for school, I didn't want to spend a dime on anything else. I lived carefully from paycheck to paycheck and my expenses were relatively few, but my paychecks weren't so fat either. I didn't know anything about the laws of abundance back then (still a learning process!).

Given my resistance (and I can resist with the tenacity of ten men holding a rope lest they be pulled into the sea) to taking the class due to finances, it took Mary's encouragement to get me to go ahead, still wearing my reluctant shoes. When I look back and see how many times I've pulled those shoes out of the closet it makes me smile at myself; each and every time I wear them the thing I am most resisting is exactly the one thing that I most need. I don't always exactly walk into the open arms of Divine guidance; sometimes I have to be dragged by the hair. This was one of those times.

Just a few hours into the class, however, I knew without a doubt in my mind that I wanted to teach others about Reiki. I was going all the way with this one. And Cristina made it so clear and so easy.

As for my fear of spending the money for the class? When I arrived there, Cristina handed me a note. It was from my friend Mary K. In the note, she congratulated me on taking the class, on learning Reiki at last. Then Cristina smiled and shared with me that Mary K had paid my tuition in full—because that's the kind of good fairy she was—and continues to be.

This simple yet profound act of kindness that my friend showed me in that moment meant more to my own sense of worth than words can ever say. Thank you, Mary K, for bringing me to Reiki and thank you, Cristina, for being my first Reiki teacher. It has shaped and transformed my life beyond recognition.

FEBRUARY 6

An outing of my own

Joe has come down with a cold, poor dear, and needs some R & R. For a man who rarely gets sick, he's had his share of it on this trip so far. So yesterday after feeding us both breakfast and seeing that he was well-settled on the couch watching his "for men only" channel or some such thing (no, it's not as exciting as it sounds. I think they play "Star Wars" movies and the like), I took myself into the village of Uppermill.

I waited for Bus 184 at Lovers Lane for 10 minutes, only to watch the bus drive right by me. I don't understand the bus system yet, but hey, it wasn't raining and it was all downhill, so off I went. (I found out later that you have to wave at the drivers for them to stop). I even saw a suggestion of sun along the way. I remembered the shortcut that Joe and I took by the river a few days previously, so I diverted to the canal path, stopping at Tesco, which was right on the way. I got some Cadbury chocolate and Turkish Delight to send home to family.

I continued along the canal into the village—a good walk, about a mile and a half maybe, but all downhill so it went quickly. I purchased a couple of cards and envelopes and had a bit of a struggle in the tiny post office juggling all of my packages and getting things sorted to mail out, but eventually succeeded. Time to attempt catching the bus again and hope it wouldn't drive past me this time. I met a nice woman and her husband, also waiting for the 184, who commiserated with me that the bus system is a mystery. Sometimes they stop and sometimes they don't; sometimes they come when the schedule indicates and sometimes they don't show up at all. That made me feel a little less mad (as in bonkers). She said it was £2.60 for bus fare. That sounds like a lot; I almost could have taken a taxi for that. But I wanted to experience the bus, which did come and did stop and turned out to be a double decker! I sat right by the door on the first floor to be sure I got dropped off at the right place. Lovers Lane was practically the first stop, but as the bus wound through and out of the village, up and up, I was so happy to be riding and not walking.

Besides, I still had the Lovers Lane footpath to go—only for the few blocks to the house, but at a very steep grade. I was determined not to stop this time. I would walk slowly and breathe really fast if I had to, but I was going to keep walking. And I made it!—out of breath, for sure, but still standing. You think I exaggerate but I do not. The hills here are truly elevating.

Not ten minutes after I arrived at the house, it began to pour. Talk about Divine timing. I liked my day out.

FEBRUARY 7

One windy Sunday

Saturday it poured all day. I don't know why they call it pouring; there are many other adjectives I could use to describe the rivers of water that flowed from the sky all afternoon and evening on Friday, and all day and night Saturday. There is something to be said for actual rain that gives one a feeling of comfort and coziness as opposed to just dreary, cloudy skies. But after 48 hours of being inside, at the first sign of clearer skies and actual sunshine, I could sit still not a moment longer.

Even now as I write this, Mr. Sun shines on my computer screen, making me squint. I can tell you, I've never appreciated him more than I have spending a winter in England. There are, in fact, many things that I have come to appreciate more fully since being here. Friends, family, learning the true meaning of home, warm houses, hot baths, the wind and the rain and the all of it. I appreciate it all. They say that a near-death experience makes one appreciate life, but I do believe that four and a half months of housesitting in another country could run a close second.

Joe's cold has now been defined by him as a sinus infection, and he declares that he will be staying in again today to rest. He has been very tired, though he didn't cough as much last night, so that is a good thing. Since I cannot convince him, nor will I even try, to go to a doctor, I am happy with the little things that he agrees to, like echinacea tea, Olbas oil on his pillow, and Vitamin C. And of course Reiki. He will always say yes to that. But his right eye looks bloodshot today (his sinus, he says) and his general condition is one of malaise.

He encouraged me quite strongly to get myself out of doors, and somewhat reluctantly, I went. Once outside I was caught up in the moment. The sun had hidden from me, and it was windy and cold, but I didn't care. I was on a new road that I hadn't walked before in a land of enchanting beauty.

Out of the house I turned left to follow a country road that also led into the village but which looked like a long way when Ava and Jack drove us that way, so we hadn't walked it yet. This particular housesit, like the one in Greenfield, is minus a car, if you haven't already noticed. And this road was going in my favorite direction. Downhill. So I decided to take it as far as I felt comfortable, and then either walk back or go all the way into the village and figure out my way home then.

This road, so typical of England, had a footpath about every 50 yards, it seemed. I think I will take a picture of every footpath sign along this road and put them together. This wonderful thing called a footpath goes through every town, in between many houses, and inevitably through farms and fields everywhere you go. I just can't get over it; I am in love with this country for walking. I could spend a lifetime just walking all the footpaths my feet could find. And in Scotland they say you can walk anywhere you want, through anyone's property, through all the fields—anywhere. Free to roam, they call it.

I was so excited that I couldn't decide which way to walk! Should I take one of the footpaths not knowing where it might lead or should I stay on the main road? I did follow one path over the hill a ways and it led to a field full of mud. I had worn my trainers (sneakers), so I turned around to walk back to the main road and all of a sudden I heard it. I was walking between two stone walls that were higher than my head, and I could hear the wind coming through the lane. It was an old wind and it was carrying voices of days and people of the past along with it. Instead of being creepy, it was so interesting to me that I stopped just to listen for a bit. A wind like this I'd never heard before.

Back at the main road and heading further in the direction of the village, I passed a man and his dog. He lives up here on a farm that sits on both sides of the road. What a life he must have. A little further along I stopped and saw the road winding ahead. I knew from this point I could turn around and walk back up to the house or I could continue forward, seeing where it took me, seeing if I could find the village. I couldn't quite decide so I asked my Higher Self. The Higher Self always knows. Yes was the answer I got. Off I went, down and down and down some more.

I saw big red cows, woolly sheep, a tiny grey and black pony with a raincoat on, three horses, and miles and miles of open fields, covered in blankets of green and brown. I don't know why parts of the Pennines are green and some are brown. I hope to get closer and find out. There are only patches of trees on these mountains; the rest is a canvas of earthy colors. And they looked so inviting to climb, unlike the rough Rocky Mountains, which I would never dream of trying to scale. Lower altitude helps.

Each turn, each dip revealed another eyeful of wonder. Before long, I arrived at the red phone box, where I recalled Ava saying to stay left there. I stayed left and came to a roundabout, not sure whether to go right or left. I thought maybe to the right, and I asked a couple walking by. They confirmed my guess, although they looked at me strangely when I asked,

"Which way leads to the downtown?"

"What?" they said. I told them, "Uppermill." "Oh," they said, and smiled. Yes, we both spoke English, just a different kind.

As I walked along now, I reached the Garden Center that my friend from the bus stop told me about on Friday. Yay! Things are happening. I'm making discoveries. Now I know we can walk here along this beautiful country road and have afternoon tea at the Garden Center. Just around the center, a man behind me asked if I had gin in my water bottle. Yes, I said, that's why I can't find where I'm going. He walked alongside me, speaking in an English accent I didn't understand at all. I asked him where he was from, and he said "Oldham."

Boy, are we in trouble when we get to Scotland! I'm told the English there is even *more* difficult to understand. For now, though, this Oldham-accented Brit told me of a nice cafe just at the next roundabout where you could sit outside and have a coffee or sandwich along the canal. "Come along," he said, "I'll walk with you." We walked about a block or so and he pointed it out and then made his way home in the other direction, tipping his hat and bidding me good day.

What a find. It's called The Limekiln and is housed in a large stone building that sits along the water, just as the man had described. I went inside to order myself a tea and a cookie to take home for Joe. The woman said she would ring me a taxi when I was ready, and I sat outside in the cold, fresh air, watching the water and enjoying my tea. I looked at the menu on the way out and was so excited to see that they had free-range eggs, veggie sausage, and lots of other tantalizing dishes for breakfast. Joe and I can walk here when he's better and have a lovely breakfast! They also have

French toast, which is one of his favorites.

The taxi service was a different one than the one we used before. It's privately owned and the driver was very kind and talkative on the way back. I took his card and let him know we will be calling him again. This one is an improvement over the one we used to go to the Old Original, though they may charge a little more. But hey, a pleasant taxi ride is worth a few extra quid.

Now I am home and writing again while Joe naps. For dinner, we will have eggplant parmesan or *aubergine* parmesan as they call it here. Tomorrow is a 2 day of the 2/5 fast. I do so hope Joe will be feeling well soon.

FEBRUARY 8

Another rainy day

It's been raining now for at least 24 hours straight. I think we've found the water fountain of the world, or at least of England. The taxi driver told me yesterday that even though the weather is lousy in this part of England, the people make up for it. I think Joe and I should get out to see more people… when he is better.

He took a long nap yesterday and then stayed up till 4 a.m. to watch the Denver Broncos win the Superbowl! Maybe not the best thing for his cold but I know it made him really happy to see the game. We had a long talk with my brother yesterday, and he and Joe spent about a half hour on the phone. Whatsapp is the greatest traveling companion you could have, well, second to Joe that is. Free calls to anywhere, anytime.

The house we are staying in is quite comfortable. It has two stories and we are sleeping upstairs, which is kind of its own little apartment in a sense, minus kitchen. It has a cozy attic-like bedroom with dormers and skylights, and 'my' meditation room with a comfy couch and chair and a TV. People are very big on their TVs over here. There is one in almost every room. We only use the one in the downstairs living room. We have a tiny bathroom with shower just next to our bed and there are three more bathrooms on the first floor. Joe has set up to use one of the downstairs bathrooms as his bathroom.

We don't poke around in our housesitting houses, though I imagine some people might do so. We are quite respectful of the homeowners' privacy and their homes and take good care of them. Our motto is to leave things better than we found them (butter dishes and bath rugs aside). People are giving us quite a show of trust to allow us to stay in their homes and take care of their pets, and we don't take that lightly.

Ava and Jack have told us to use all their spices and such freely and to have a dig through to find what we need. And I love this part—seeing what people stock in their cupboards for cooking. In this case, they are very well-prepared, and I was grateful for bicarbonate of soda, vanilla, cinnamon, and nutmeg this morning as I made Joe a batch of his super cookies. It was a difficult thing to do as I am on a fast day of the 5/2 diet, but I made them just after porridge so I wasn't too tempted by them. I asked him not to do the diet today or any day until he is fully well again. He's only eaten three of his cookies so far and went back to sleep off his Super Bowl hangover.

There is a garage in this house that is accessed by going downstairs, so it almost feels like a basement. This is where the kitties have their litterbox, and the washing machine is at the bottom of the stairs. High up in the stairwell there hangs four wooden slats suspended on ropes. When you want to dry your laundry, you let this contraption down by loosening the rope where it is tied on the wall. Then you carefully drape the laundry on the slats (an art in itself) and pull on the rope to suspend your clothes high in the air. I've hung clothes many times before but never this way!

The living room boasts the wall of glass, showing us daily the Pennines across the valley to the north. On the rare occasion that the sun has shown up here so far, it becomes a glorious view, although it even looks nice in the rain. The kitchen has large windows and a lovely view of the small garden, chicken house and chickens, and the hill beyond that leads to Scouthead, home of the Old Original. The beauty of this place is truly unending.

We are trying to decide where we can go for Valentine's Day dinner this weekend. I am trusting Joe will be better and ready to get out of the house!

Tonight—grilled salmon for dinner along with tomato/lentil soup for Joe. Mmmm… can't wait to taste those cookies tomorrow when the fast day is over.

FEBRUARY 9

Here comes the Sun

Today we woke up to clouds but no rain! Joe was still feeling poorly, and we discussed the possibility of him seeing a doctor. Interesting how much more vulnerable you can allow yourself to feel in another country. But since neither of us would go to the doctor if we were home, we didn't worry overly much. This flu has been taking its time to develop and hasn't cleared as quickly as either of us thought it would.

I started the morning sharing Reiki with Joe and then he got up and went out to clean the chicken coop and put out the trash. He was making an effort to get rid of his sickness by going out in the "fresh," damp, cold air. The chickens were happy and checked out their freshly cleaned home, but Joe was about done in by the time he was finished. He laid on the couch and closed his eyes, and I, realizing this was going to be another day of rest for Joe, put on my coat and left to get some supplies for our temporary home.

Once again, I bypassed the bus and walked down into the village. I mailed off three packages and cards for Valentine's Day to family back home, with two pretty bookmarks for my daughters. It cost me the equivalent of $23 to mail three envelopes that contained about $9 worth of goods. It was worth it because it's so fun to get something mailed to you from overseas. But most things I will be carrying home in April, unless we have more bags than hands by that time.

I checked out a restaurant in Uppermill for Valentine's dinner, but didn't like the ambience of the place, at least not for a romantic meal. Then I realized how foolish an idea it is anyway when Joe is still sick. Valentine's Day may well be spent cuddling on the couch if he feels better, and that will be just fine with me. I just feel excited because there are more places to eat here than any other sit we've been on so far—interesting places. And I love to try new things. It's not so much about the eating but about the adventure of it all.

I so enjoyed my walk into the village, even though I hated leaving Joe at first, but I knew that he would just rest while I was gone and we needed some basic items. As soon as I was out of the house, I remembered how good it was for me. I stopped at the butcher's shop and got a small whole chicken to make bone broth and homemade chicken soup. It helped Joe feel better last time, so I thought it worth a try. The butcher explained to me why he doesn't sell free-range chickens (bird flu). I also bought Joe some bacon that looks more like fatty ham slices. He will love it when his appetite returns.

It was a good walk from the village back to the Tesco along the river, and just before I descended the steps to the river, a group of bikers crossed in front of me. They appeared to be a fun, 60-something group out for some exercise together, and one man stopped in his tracks, turned to look at me, and said hello as if he'd never seen a woman before. The group was all men, except for one woman. Another man turned, pointed to his bicycle seat, and said, "You can sit right here and come along!" It brightened my day and just made me laugh, turning the eyes of the 60s set! But then again, maybe they don't know how old they are any more than I do!

The weather was holding nicely until I got to the Tesco. The store was blissfully uncrowded, and so I relaxed and moseyed around, slowly picking out everything we needed. Most of the stores I've been to in Britain are usually packed with people and you can hardly move, much less see anything on the shelves. So this was really pleasant. I stocked up on orange juice and some other things for Joe, and some veggies and hummus, rice crackers, etc., for me.

I decided to do the self-checkout and see if it was as annoying as at home. And it turned out not to be! I spent 53 quid and I pushed my cart over to customer service to ask her to ring for a taxi. I gave her the number and the address.

Once outside, I noticed the ground was now wet and the taxi driver, who arrived like magic, told me it had been snowing. I'd missed it. I was so happy to have found the Gold Medal Cab Company here in Saddleworth. I felt like I was riding in style and not only did the driver help with getting the groceries into the car; he helped me carry them up the steep driveway as well. They say you aren't supposed to tip, but that kind of service is surely worth a quid or two!

Joe was happy to see me. His appetite has gone downhill today, probably since the cold/cough turned to fever/cold/cough. Rest and fluids, says my BFFL Sharon, who is also a nurse. I talked to her on the phone today to ask her about his symptoms.

The afternoon passed pleasantly with some sunshine while I was sitting on the couch doing some work for the writing workshop. I planned to get out again to walk, but first I went upstairs to check on Joe and give him some Reiki. By the time I got back downstairs, the day had turned to light rain. After a bit, I closed the chicken coop for the night along with the cat door and started to think about making dinner. Bone broth had been in the making for several hours already, and I convinced Joe to put an onion pack on his chest.

I could almost see my Dad beside me as I spooned the onions and a little of the juice onto paper towels and wrapped them in a tea towel for his chest. My Dad was king of the onion pack, and used to try to persuade us to also drink the onion juice, which I hated. But I can tell you that the onion pack on the chest has cured me many a time from a very bad chest cold, thanks to Pap, as we called him.

After watching (with eyes half-closed) "Star Trek" and "Pickers," Joe went off to bed. I could hear him coughing from downstairs while I typed. Tomorrow my efforts will continue with nursing care for Joe, yoga, walking, continuing with my writing, and having an Indian head massage! Another full day on Millionaire's Row.

FEBRUARY 10

What I am learning through writing

I am learning the ways to discovering myself are many and there are an infinite number of paths that lead to *me*. I have moved beyond all the excuses about not writing. And this writing is discovering the creative effort—not creating something simply on my own, but joining the flow of everything that already is. And I smile as I realize Source is the creative power behind the work, behind the words.

The journey to get to her, to the Divine part of me that creates, is fraught with obstacles and challenges. All of the challenges are made of and by myself. First is the challenge of, am I good enough? Or can I make time for this so-called writing, because to make time for it means making myself important to me. Or to put it another way, can I put myself first to access the Divine in me. It also requires announcing to the world that I am making writing a priority. Then, as unbelievable as it seems, I will have to sometime, somewhere, show my work to someone else to read.

For years this felt so very scary, as if I were exposing myself nakedly on a stage for all to see my flaws and imperfections. I remember my first writing group about 20 years ago and how shy I was to share my work with these three other wonderful women. Writing has been an on again, off again love affair for me, one which I believe has always been in direct relationship to my sense of self-worth. With age can indeed come wisdom and also a sense of one's self, and it makes me happy to look back and realize that, even during my off-again phases with writing, I was still maturing in a way that would eventually support its fruition. Now I am not afraid to shine.

Facing the challenges of sending out the work for publication, and learning to call myself a writer and then actually believe it were my next hurdles. It took a very long time to jump over them, but suddenly I was there with the help of my writing coach, Alissa, and my own growth. I'd reached the goal I didn't know I was seeking; I am a writer!

And then came the time to look at the reasons why I was a writer who didn't write: Because I lacked talent? Because I lacked time? Because I was lacking? *Lack: the state of being without or not having enough of something.*

I looked at other writers and I compared. They were so good, so much better than I. But how was that possible, because we are all made of the same stuff. We are all energy, and it is into this energy that we flow and mingle, until we learn to join with that which is writing. We all have access.

So excuses be gone. I sit with the work, and within that work lies judgment itself. What shall I write? Even as I sit down to pen and paper I do not know. Alissa says write what you see. She gives me little signposts to follow as if I am going into a dense forest and do not know the way through. I can only see a little bit, and so I write a little. And then the next day a little more until so many words come forth onto the page that I cannot stop. I think it's bad; I hear her saying in my head, "Keep writing. It's okay to write a really bad first draft."

What does that mean? Doesn't it have to be good to mean something? No. It doesn't. All it must do is exist in form on paper, to go from the workings of my heart to the pen and then authentically to the page. And then, in some perfectly magical way, if I can make the clay and I can mold it a little, and the next day I mold it some more and add more clay to it, eventually a form will appear and it will have magic and it will be something. Something that has been created by the Divine part of me that lives. To the work, to the glorious work.

FEBRUARY 11

The ups and the downs

Today was one of those days in which my age changed all throughout the day. When I first got up, I felt at least 90, as neither Joe nor I got much sleep. His nighttime cough had us both up and I had made him a 2 a.m. onion pack. He finally drifted back to sleep in the early morning hours and I did too, only to be awoken at 6:15 by one hungry cat I have started calling

Morris. He reminds me of that cat.

To say I got up on the wrong side of the bed would be an understatement and also a pretty rare occurrence. I am very fortunate to be one of those people who gets up fully awake and has never needed coffee. This morning, however, was a little different. Joe, on the other hand, arose feeling energetic. I didn't do morning meditation and yoga, and my peace of mind certainly noticed!

I made us both some porridge while Joe went out to open the chicken coop. He helped me with a few chores, but by the time breakfast was over, his energy was already spent. Even though it was only just after breakfast, we both stretched out on the couches and put on a Harry Potter movie. I fell asleep for a good while, and though Joe rested, he only slept a few minutes.

The morning, which started out cloudy, had turned to bright sunshine, and I made the decision to walk to the village to get Joe some cough medicine. We spoke again about him going to the 24-hour clinic in Ashton, but he wanted to wait a few more days.

I left for the village about 12:30 and waved to handyman Felix as I passed by him just down the road. We'd called him to repair the automatic door on the chicken coop. The day felt so warm that I knew my puffy coat would end up being too much, but I was already on my way. Down, down the hill I went, enjoying the air and the intermittent sunshine very much indeed. Now I felt 35!

I went to the pharmacy and was delighted to find that the pharmacist, instead of being trapped behind a counter filling prescriptions, was front and center in the little store and wanted to know all of Joe's symptoms, which now included a sore ear. He recommended not one but two different cough medicines, one for day and one for night. He said that the virus going around is a very nasty one and that it is taking a long time to get over. He himself had it for five weeks. I decided I wouldn't share this with Joe, because I didn't want him to get discouraged.

My spirits were so high (feeling more like a 20 year old now) that I began to explore the town with new eyes. I ventured into a corner sandwich shop and decided to get something there for Joe that might inspire a little appetite. He hasn't been eating much. I bought him a tuna sandwich on a brown muffin with butter (he loves tuna salad and hasn't had it for a long while) and a chocolate cupcake. If the tuna didn't tempt him the chocolate certainly would.

Armed with a bag full of cough medicine magic, sandwich, and cupcake, I practically skipped along the sidewalk. I stopped briefly at the bus stop to look at the schedule, felt the warm air still on my skin with no sign of rain, and decided to go for it, walking up the long hill this time. I was tired of paying for taxis and buses.

My 20-year-old status definitely started to advance as I walked up the long hill home, especially after I stopped at the Tesco and added a large bottle of orange juice to my load of parcels. I was in my 40s by the time I reached Farrars pub, about halfway to home, and my pace got slower. By the time I reached the first footpath to traverse the really steep part of the journey, I felt at least 70. When I reached our doorstep, sweating and heart pounding, I thought, well maybe 50. After all, aerobic exercise is good for you, and besides, I hadn't even attempted to walk up from the village before so this was definitely progress!

I got Joe started on his cough medicine, and eventually he ate his tuna sandwich and a little chicken broth. Time will tell, and we will keep looking for the up side.

FEBRUARY 12

A break in the road

Today was a good day—eventful, surely. It all started last night, after I gave Joe a dose of nighttime cough medicine that I bought him. He was running a nighttime fever again, and I gave him two paracetamol as well (same as Advil, I believe). A few minutes later, he was lying in bed, talking gibberish. Not like he was sleeping, either. Just telling me things about the numbers of the rooms where we were staying and how we needed to sort out the rooms, etc. I suddenly got worried that maybe I'd given him too much cough syrup.

I left him counting rooms and snuck downstairs to read the bottle again. The dosage was confusing; it said to give 3 x 5ml per time. To me that meant 15ml, which is what I gave him. But given the fact that everything is so different here and that I kept reading the large black print that said DO NOT GIVE MORE THAN THE RECOMMENDED DOSE, I decided to go onto the website for the walk-in center that was recommended to us. There I found a directive to call 111 for non-emergency, after-hour questions. I spoke to the woman at length and she assured me that I didn't give him too much medication. Whew! That at least was a relief. Then she asked to speak to him.

By this time, he was sitting up and totally lucid, and able to answer all her questions. Based on her assessment, she said that we needed to go to the walk-in center within 24 hours and gave us the address. He might have been reluctant before, but since the nurse on the phone told him to go to the clinic, he would do it. Joe lay back down and started mumbling incoherencies but soon fell asleep.

This morning, we left just after 8:00 with our Gold Medal cab driver for the town of Oldham and the care clinic. Arriving early was smart, as there was hardly any wait. We saw a wonderful nurse practitioner named Trudy who assessed Joe and pretty quickly told him that he had tonsillitis! No wonder the onion pack and chicken soup hadn't worked. I was so happy and also very relieved when she told us that his chest was clear and that we could get the prescribed antibiotic at the pharmacy right next door. While we were still in the office with Trudy, Joe mentioned that my eye was looking sore. The night before my eye got itchy and raw on the lid when my "Morris" decided to lie on my chest for a while. He likes to cuddle. Trudy suggested that I go out and register with the nurse so she could look at me, too! And so I did. Trudy told me that it might be an allergic reaction to the cats, recommending an antihistamine and some eyedrops. I have always suspected that I was a bit allergic to cats! And we have two more cat-sits. But I'm not that allergic; I just have to be careful about letting them lie on me. I like to think I could build up a tolerance though, because they are so sweet.

Due to Britain's NHS (National Healthcare System), we didn't pay a dime for either visit! We were treated very thoughtfully, given kind attention and good advice, and practically no wait. Our first impression of the NHS was very positive.

We taxied home. Joe was tired and stretched out for a rest while I did some writing and website work. After a few hours, he was rested enough to take a walk with me. We took another new footpath that I found yesterday on my way home. It led us up over the fields, revealing incredible views above us to the top of the hills and the sheep grazing at the top of the rise, and the village and river below. We could look straight across at the Pennines on the other side of the village, miles away. I imagined it was similar to the walks James Herriot used to take across the moors.[12]

We traversed across the path for a good while, reluctantly turning back toward our home away from home. Joe's legs got a little shaky a few times from being sick and not having walked for so many days, and I wondered about the wisdom of such a big walk for him so soon. But it did his heart good. He was tired when we returned but happy to have been out.

Trudy had told us that he should be feeling much better within 48 hours and that he should take it fairly easy for about a week. All in all, I'm feeling much gratitude for friendly people, Joe's diagnosis and treatment, our beautiful surroundings, and another beautiful day. Life is truly good to us and we are so taken care of, despite some bumps along the way.

---

[12] James Alfred "Alf" Wight Herriot, aka James Herriot on his book jackets, was a well-known veterinary surgeon who wrote All Creatures Great and Small and other stories about his life as a vet in Yorkshire after World War II.

FEBRUARY 13

Britain in July

In July and August, at least in the northern part of England and in Scotland, the sun stays out till 11:30 at night and comes back up at 3 a.m.! The next time we visit the UK, I hope it will be in summer.

Today, I am returning to my ever-growing list of observations I've made about being in this country. Everyone has a definite opinion about everything; because of that, if you ask two people about the same thing, you will probably get two very different answers. I am the type of person who likes to ask questions—always have. I remember one time as a little girl firing questions at my Dad, who was trying to have a little nap after work (he liked to sit back in his easy chair for a little bit before dinner) and him squinting through one eye and telling me that I should be a reporter when I grew up.

I'm still asking questions, especially on this trip. I ask people what they think about this town or that, where they like to eat most—the things visitors always ask. And in reply, one person will say this pub has the best food and another will say he or she would never eat there. Two people have told us to go to Manchester and mooch about! They said there's lots of good shopping and eating there. Then two other people shared, "Avoid Manchester at all costs. You don't want to go there." One person says that Scotland will be beautiful and you will love it, while the next person says, "You're going to Scotland? It awful there—rains all the time and is bloody cold."

So I just keep asking, and when not asking, just listening because the English love to tell you about their country once they learn you are a visitor, which they know as soon as you open your mouth. Or sometimes you just have to walk into a place and they've already tagged you a foreigner. I cannot tell you how many times we've been asked if we are Canadians—just yesterday, in fact, by the taxi driver. But nonetheless there's no mistaking that you're not from 'round here.

Joe woke up feeling, as he said, about 85 percent today! Hip, hip hooray! I, on the other hand, was a bit rough this morning, though I think it's just thermal inversion; we woke to a heavy fog over the land. It is now clearing and getting brighter and I have finished my meditation and self-Reiki and am picking up speed.

This afternoon brought me a long country lane walk into the village to make reservations for a Valentine's lunch. I stopped at the Garden Center. What a jewel of a place. It's a feast for the senses, with pretty pots of flowers and bushes outside for sale—in February! Things seem to grow year round here. They have an indoor shop with lovely jams and other pretty things for sale and a little cafe where they serve afternoon tea. It's a full tea, which means you can get a sandwich or scones or crumpets with it. We shall definitely do this one day.

Just down the road from the Garden Center is the Limekiln, the little cafe I discovered during Joe's illness and have been dreaming about going to ever since. I was greeted by a lovely young waitress who booked us in for a 3 p.m. reservation on Sunday, Valentine's Day. Perfect. We'll be able to get a sandwich or dessert; Joe can have a beer if he wants or even a glass of wine, though I doubt he will be ready for it. But nonetheless, the food looks terrific, he can order a small amount if he likes, and if it's nice enough, we can sit outside and watch the canal flow by! At one time the canal was used as a means to deliver the wool from the sheep farms on the surrounding hills.

Joe still has little appetite so this is the perfect solution for our Valentine's Day—no three-course meal for us, just a nice time out. We will walk the country road in if he feels up for it and take a taxi home. Or we can taxi both ways.

It is beginning to stay light later each day and the kittens sit for longer periods watching outdoors, even though they can go out whenever they like. I think they just like watching the world as they know it. They are becoming much friendlier with us now, coming into our bedroom and the living room more often and talking more. Mufasa talks a bit too much sometimes, especially at 5:45 a.m. but then he is named after a lion. Getting up early is good, Mufasa says.

FEBRUARY 14

Let life happen

It's another day in which the sun decided to grace us with its presence. It never appears alone without its clouds. Instead, it likes to play hide and seek with us, saying catch me if you can. I dawdled in the morning, though, taking my time getting started, and we shared Valentine's cards. I made Joe a bacon and egg sandwich for breakfast. Two eggs and bacon! The man was hungry! Cheers!

I did some yoga while the sun streamed through the windows and it finally coaxed me outside. I wandered up over the hill leading to the Old Original and the wind was cold, while the sun now played peekaboo with the clouds. Such a beautiful walk! The fields stretched out before me, wide and green and rolling down a gentle hill, each field separated by stone walls inviting me through one type or another of a pass-through. I walked about halfway to the Old Original and then turned back towards my beloved, resting at home.

On my way back through the fields, I thought about the conversation that Joe and I shared that morning. We are at a pivotal point in our lives right now, perhaps more so than some ever have to face.

It's been abundantly clear since we've been here in England that being at sea level is much easier for us both. Although Joe has had a few sicknesses while here, overall he says that he feels much more energy. I realized in how many ways I feel better, as was brought home to me yesterday when I took a four and a half mile walk, half of it uphill, and came home not even tired.

All of this seems to be leading to us moving to another place, but the questions are how, where, and when. How do we move farther away from our daughters? And, in fact, which direction do we go? What about Joe's family and friends back east? Do we make this move as soon as we return? Do we wait a while? And more importantly, how, where, and when can we best serve the Divine purpose that lies in our hearts? Following Divine purpose has always been number one for me, whether that purpose was raising children, caring for horses, writing, doing massage therapy, teaching Reiki, and the many, many things in between and all around.

So as I walked this field hand-in-hand with the Divine, surrounded by Mother Earth in all of her shining glory, I asked, "What's next? Can you show me? Will you please show me?" then stopped to sit on some rocks in the field, the sun lighting up the left side of my face, hoping for some wise reply. And within just a few hours, during our much anticipated Valentine's Day lunch, one answer came through very clearly.

We left the house on Millionaire's Row in the late morning, walking the country road towards the Limekiln instead of taking a taxi as Joe was feeling well enough to do so. The sun was now officially hiding behind the clouds but that was okay. The air was brisk and we enjoyed our long walk down the country lane. It was so great to share this walk with Joe for the first time. We went into the Garden Center first and looked all around. He was impressed.

We arrived at the Limekiln about a half hour early, so we decided to walk the footpath along the canal toward Uppermill Village—a glorious walk that was being enjoyed by many people and their dogs. Ducks and geese swam along beside us, waiting for crusts of bread. After about 15 minutes, we turned to go back to the restaurant, where they had a table for two in the corner reserved just for us. I told Joe then, what more could we ask for on Valentine's Day, or any other day? We toasted to our first Valentine's across the ocean.

We shared a great meal and when it was time to decide on dessert, I splurged on the chocolate cake! (tomorrow is a fast day, so my tummy will be extra growly). Joe got up and walked to the counter to look at the cookies and I wanted to go after him, to tell him to sit down and make sure the waitress got his order. And in that moment, I heard a voice in my head say, "Let life happen!" And I smiled, for oh how easy it was to do just that, once I knew. I watched him speak to a few of the waitresses and when he came back to the table, no words needed to be said. He'd ordered his cookie from the counter and got it alongside mine.

So simple, you say. This was so obvious. And yet the bigger message became clear to me only now. *Let life happen* was a message straight from the Divine about the unknown future that lies ahead of us.

So for now, here's to keeping eyes wide open, staying in a state of listening and …you guessed it, letting life happen.

FEBRUARY 15

Getting to know the neighbors

One thing that stands out on this sit that is different from the rest is that we haven't met any of the neighbors, nor have we met anyone out walking (as in Seaton) or at the pubs. Of course a large part of that is simply because we haven't been out much at all, due to Joe's tonsillitis, etc. But, all in all, it's a different sort of place in that way. More spread out. The hill we are on is almost like a suburb of sorts.

So this morning, on another gloriously sunny day (so very, very blessed), we set out to follow a new footpath, the one that Joe now calls the whispering walls, because it was the very footpath where I discovered the stone walls that seemed to speak to me on the wind. We decided to take the whispering walls under further investigation. The walls stayed with us for a good long stretch, which was quite an advantage, since the wind was not whispering today; it was shouting.

The cold air felt invigorating though and by the time we reached the open field, it died down for a little bit. We climbed over a staircase of stone steps laid into the wall as a travel-through spot and entered the land of our neighbors—four-legged neighbors in the form of sheep—hundreds of them on the hillsides, filling one field to the next. I couldn't tell if Joe was hesitating to enter the field due to the sheep, but I climbed up and over and proceeded up the road, heading straight for them.

I reasoned that if they were dangerous there wouldn't be a footpath, and there were no signs saying, "Beware Sheep" like the one sign that said, "Beware, Bull in Field" on the way to the Old Original.

It was clear, though, that these sheep weren't used to two-leggeds walking through their midst. They looked at us like party crashers and promptly scuttled out of the way as we approached. We calmly walked through them, up to the crest of a hill that we hoped would hold an expansive view.

All the views here are beautiful, but this time we'd found quite possibly the highest view of all on this side of the hills from which you could look down at Uppermill, the river, and the whole panoramic view of the

Pennines. Combined with the crystal sunshine, being there left us silent and staring, taking it all in, reverently, humbly. I tried to use the panorama shot on my camera but soon gave in to just being there. When we got our fill of sheer beauty, we turned back for our route home, which was blissfully all downhill, thank you very much! This is a walk we will take again, so a word to the wise, dear sheep. We don't plan to be strangers.

FEBRUARY 17

All in a day's Sit

It is astounding to me all that can happen in 24 hours. Days in our lives can tend to just slip away or drone on the same as the ones before if we don't happen to take notice. I love and appreciate my ability to jump into life wanting to experience every moment, but I also have those days that pass unnoticed by me, like anyone else. I promise myself right here and now that I will not have another one of those for as long as I am given.

What that means, really, is that my job is to find the meaning in each and every day (eventually every moment, but let's start with a manageable macrocosm and work our way to the microcosm, since it is all the same anyway), even if that day seems ordinary, dull, boring, scary, troublesome, painful, or filled with worry. Each and every one of us has had one or more of those days that we could describe as one or all of the above. The day, in fact, is created in our minds, not in our outer circumstances. Given the same exact circumstances, two people could have a completely different experience, as we well know!

Take the last 24 hours, for example. They were filled with fun, ordinary events, worry and the like, all in the space of one day. The morning began with me getting ready for an outing to get my hair done. Meanwhile, Joe was talking with Felix, the maintenance man downstairs, who'd stopped by to discuss the problem with the electronic timer that regulates the closing of the chicken coop door at night. Thankfully, Ava and Jack had given us Felix's number in case we had any troubles at the house.

Although troubles with the house have been few, Felix has come round several times, and he and Joe have been having some nice chats each time. This morning, Felix invited us to visit a "few pubs" with him and his wife on the Sunday coming if we have "nought" to do. Just after I wrote yesterday that we hadn't made any friends yet on this sit in Grasscroft, the Universe laughed at me once again. It happens all the time. I call it Reverse Manifestation! The Divine has the ability to give us everything we need, and is really and truly there to help us in every way. So even if we are asking in a "it's never going to happen" kind of way, the Universe can hear the request and make it happen. "I don't think we are ever going to make friends" was heard as "We are going to make friends; we have made friends." It is of course always more powerful to state things in the positive form of an affirmation, but I've had this happen to me so many times that I know it works this way too. It's as though the Universe is having a bit of a joke on me, showing me how easy it all really is—if I would but ask.

I walked into the village early, around 9:30, and it was quite cold and blowy. But I enjoyed the walk thoroughly. I felt, not for the first time, the beauty of taking myself on my own two feet. I arrived a few minutes early at Kay's Kut 'n Kurl in Uppermill with my bag of hair color in tow. Kay was to be my hairdresser that day. She kindly agreed to use the color I'd brought from the States and also give me a trim for 37 quid. A fair price, I thought, and there was a lovely irony to it. She used 37 ml of liquid to make the color stay in, we left it on for 37 minutes, and I paid her 37 quid. I love the beauty and synchronicity of numbers.

As I sat with color on my hair, I struck up a conversation with an older woman named Rita, who'd worked at that shop for 30-plus years. "I've known Kay since she was 16 and just starting out in the business. Now she owns the place," Rita said proudly. Rita was a curiosity to me. I couldn't guess her age, but she might have been in her 70s. She was dressed impeccably in a pale pink sweater outfit with a white collar, and, by way of her dress, I wouldn't have even guessed she worked there until she came over to put on my plastic gown. We talked non-stop for 37 minutes while my color set, mostly about America and how she loved it there, especially Washington D.C. where she had a brother.

I noticed that Kay catered to older women and the feeling in the shop was one of caring and kindness. Joe had walked into the village and came into the shop just before I finished, so he got a chance to meet the crew. The women suggested a few places we might like to visit while we were in the area.

We walked from the shop along the canal to the Lymekiln for a very brisk open air lunch on the outdoor patio overlooking the canal. It's the first time I've ever eaten at a restaurant with my gloves on. But I loved every minute of it, and we so enjoyed our *al fresco* lunch of baked Camembert with crusty bread and apple chutney, cauliflower and almond soup, and the most delicious chocolate cake I've eaten since I had my mother's chocolate cake as a little girl. Joe enjoyed a hot tea and I a glass of their house red. (So, not a fasting day!) We called for a taxi home, as it was cold and we were ready to be back at the house, plus I didn't want Joe to push it too much. The fact that he'd walked into the village and then all around was a good sign of his strength coming back into his legs. Hooray!

Back at our temporary home, we spent the rest of the day reading and watching TV. The wind stirred up the rain, which continued all night long.

FEBRUARY 18TH

How many ways can you lose a cat?

Next morning I came downstairs to find Joe already up. He asked me about Sarafina, our shy girl cat. Had I seen her? No, I replied. He'd looked all through the house and couldn't find her. The night before, he shut the cat door and told me he'd seen her on the bed, and neither of us took much notice of her after that. She likes to lie in the back bedroom on Ava's coats at night. We don't see her much at night usually, except when Joe checks on her and pets her on his way to the downstairs bathroom, the one he is using as his man bathroom.

So the next morning, we both started to retrace our steps. You did this, I did that, where is Sarafina? We both tried to ward off a sense of "oh, no, what have we done?" and subsequent visions of her being left outside all night in the wind and rain and possibly getting eaten by a fox? I pushed those thoughts away as we both grabbed our rain gear and began to search outside around the house for her. I even walked up the hill behind the house and spoke to a neighbor. He hadn't seen her. I kept getting the nagging feeling that of course she was in the house somewhere! This was just stress and panic setting in, overcoming all logic. I remembered seeing her when I had gotten a snack around 8 p.m.

In a little while, we were both inside the house again. I'd searched all the cupboards in the kitchen and the drawers in the bedroom where she sleeps just in case somehow she'd gotten in them. And I searched the basement once more as well. As is my way, when I can't do anything about something, I proceed as if everything is normal, and so I made a piece of toast and sat at the kitchen table to eat it. Joe disappeared into his man bathroom and moments later I heard him talking from the front bedroom. "How in the world did you get in there?" and out came Sarafina to the kitchen for her breakfast. She was in the bedroom all night in the closet above the set of drawers. We could then see how she could push open the too-full closet with her paw and slip inside. Joe then remembered seeing Mufasa and Sarafina hissing at one another (as they tend to do) earlier that evening in the bedroom. Mufasa doesn't usually invade that space of hers, so our guess was that she hid in the closet to avoid him!

Relief spelled one hundred ways flooded us. Our feeling of having done something wrong left us; Sarafina had been safe all the time. What a strange way to start the day. I think it was the Universe playing a cosmic joke on us for patting ourselves on the back when Ava sung our praises, saying the cats and chickens would love us so much they wouldn't want us to leave. Beware, dear Ego, beware.

FEBRUARY 20

You never know what you are going to get

Our days are marked completely by the weather. Wednesday, our tentative plans to go to the Ashton market were waylaid by the rain, which visited us all the day. Thursday morning we got ready to catch the 9:37 train to Ashton, but walked outside to find a sheet of ice on the sidewalk as thin as a fingernail and very slippery. After clutching the wall and slip sliding to the bottom of the driveway, we decided to wait an hour.

At 10 we set off for the walk to the station. We made it easily with 10 minutes to spare. Ashton is just three train stops away, and we were there in 12 minutes. I'd made up a map so we could find the Arcade shops and the Market Hall, but it was all laid out just in front of us. So easy! We found the Super Drug and went on to Market Hall.

The historic market in Ashton[13] is said to be one of the most popular in the northeast region of the UK. I'd been to this market with Ava, and I was excited to share it with Joe. I noticed it was much more crowded than the last time as we walked about looking at all the food stalls, deciding what we wanted and where we would make our purchases. We filled our bags with fresh cheese and creamy yellow butter, fresh-baked bread and rolls, butcher's burgers for Joe, gorgeous plaice fillets, lots of veggies, blueberries

---

13 www.tameside.gov.uk/ashton/market.

and plums, and two different slices of chocolate cake (strictly for comparing and contrasting purposes).

Now back at the station, we realized that we had about 40 minutes to wait. But the sun was warm, so we sat on a bench soaking up the rays while I ate my piece of cake, licking my fingers all the while. It wasn't nearly as good as the Limekiln's, but perhaps I should have another slice there just to be certain. Nice way to diet.

An elderly man came up and started to spin his tale for us. It turned out that he was a former engineer, and he told us about some of his travels, the highlight of which was when he went on a 21-day bus tour in New Zealand. He said there was nothing like it and that we should go sometime and see that beautiful country. What a grand big world it is.

When we got back to Greenville station, we walked down to the Tesco to round off our shopping expedition and by then, laden with bags, we decided to call a taxi for the ride up the hill. The man who picked us up remembered me from the other day and we had a nice chat. He told us that the weather in Uppermill tended to have a mind of its own—that the weather here was different than everywhere else. I guess that's because of the hills and valleys here. The sun was shining when he dropped us off and when we commented on it, he said, "Enjoy it now. You never know what you are going to get."

The next day we had a walk into the village to return my library book and print out our train itineraries for future travel. Again the sun was trying to come out on the walk down, but it turned to drizzle by the time we reached the village. Lucky for us, we made it home before it started to rain in earnest. It was a fasting day for me, and I was doing all right. We enjoyed our plaice fish for dinner and I didn't even mind when Joe ate his cookies. We stayed up rather late watching a movie, but I made sure to wring the sponge of the day by squeezing in a few minutes for writing, meditation, and yoga before bed. I have been feeling bright even when it rains, feeling more energy than I've had for a long time. I don't know if my body is truly responding well to the lower altitude, but I certainly feel different.

Today we started talking about "what's up next" if we decide to move from Colorado. From our conversation, I made an initial "what we'd like to find in a place where we would live next" list, and already we have some locations that we might look at. It felt somewhat surreal later on when one of our Buena Vista friends contacted us via Skype. Our conversation reminded us of the affection we have for the town and its people who have taken us in so warmly. That reminder led us to make a phone call to Sara, another friend from BV, who said we have been gone way too long and when are we coming back.

All of this leads my heart back to its question of how to live in one "someplace" and be close to everyone we love in so many other places? It's impossible of course, considering how mobile and spread apart we all are these days. It's a question, it would seem, that has no good answer, but somehow I still want to try.

Joe's new friend Felix stopped by to firm up our plan for tomorrow. He's a really nice guy. He seems put out that we don't have a car and offered to take us to a few places this week. As he put it, it's his slow time and he's "mooching about" anyhow. Tomorrow he and his wife Isobel will pick us up at noon to go for a drive, and then we have reservations at 3 at a nice little pub that does Sunday food. Sunday dinner out is a big deal here in the UK, just like fresh flowers in your front window. It's what people do. I like it because it makes Sunday seem like a special day of the week; almost like when we were kids, and it really was special—when stores closed down and people went to church and cooked Sunday dinners and sat on their porch. Felix said that the missus had been asking all manner of questions about us, and he had told her, "Wait till tomorrow. It will give you something to talk about."

He told us a funny story about the time they went to Australia and the people they were visiting drove them 50 miles to a fish and chip shop! Felix said he hates fish and chips, so he was astounded that the people thought nothing of driving 50 miles to get it.

As we reached the end of another beautiful day on our adventure, we went upstairs to our loft bedroom with its skylights and lay in bed looking up at the clouds fly past our window, on their way in from the Irish Sea. It makes me long for Ireland, what I think of as my true home. As much as I love the UK, and I truly do, the first time I landed in Ireland, in 1988, I knew I was home. It was the kind of feeling that lets you know you've lived before. That feeling of somehow having experienced it, having smelled the smells, seen the scenery, worked the land, even though you know you haven't. Don't worry, Ireland. I'll be back to see you again. Sweet dreams.

FEBRUARY 22

Time out with Felix and Isobel

Yesterday was chucking rain once more. Felix laughed when I said it was even raining sideways. They had a little Volkswagen, and it was a cozy, rainy ride as we toured the villages in the area. We got out twice to look at the moors, even though the weather didn't allow us to see very far. Felix kept saying, "You have got to have a car here. You could see so much more."

We ended up stopping at the Swan in nearby Dobcross, a quaint old pub with red velvet chairs and a cozy fire. We sat for a long time near the fire while the guys drank a beer or two. Isobel was the DD, so she had nothing, and I had a half a glass of beer before I switched to water. Felix scoffed at me… drinking water in a pub! He said, "We won't be getting you drunk, now will we?" to which I smiled and said no. After all, I hadn't eaten since breakfast and I'm not much for drinking on an empty stomach.

It was great to spend time with Felix and Isobel, and we decided that we would stay and have our Sunday meal right there at the Swan, instead of going to the other place that they were going to take us to. And it was quite a meal. To begin, Joe and I shared a Stilton tart with red pear and walnut salad that was absolutely scrumptious. He had a blue cheese burger, and I ordered the cheese and onion pie that the elderly woman who lives down the street still makes for the restaurant. The owner said you couldn't stop her from making these pies if you tried. So, they bring her the ingredients, they pay her, and she makes them.

And I think it is becoming one of my favorite dishes here in the UK. Cheese is good in my book, served any way at all, and the cheese here has such good strong flavor. But the combination of the delicate pie crust, made to perfection, and the onion too—yum. It may not be five-star French cuisine, but it will definitely do. A really delicious salad and chips came with it, though after the tart, the slice of onion pie was about all I could eat.

We spoke to Felix and Isobel about our Reiki practice when the conversation came around to "What do you do?" and the reception was the same polite response we've gotten from most everyone here, with the exception of Ava and the woman in the pub who was a Reiki Master. Felix quite openly and kindly explained that the Brits, well, they tended to be skeptical and they needed to have things proven to them. But we remain hopeful and continue to spread the knowledge of it as best we can, even in the face of skepticism. And Isobel was just as sweet as could be. What a very nice couple indeed and very kind of them to take us out for a meal.

I miss the part of my Reiki that involves interaction with others and think I will begin to work on my Reiki teacher's manual, as it will keep me thinking even more about Reiki. I still believe that our time here is meant for a special purpose for both of us, and part of that is our transition to our new life, wherever that may be. To better health, to our new home for teaching and sharing Reiki, and to new work for Joe. There are many changes ahead for us.

FEBRUARY 24

Moving through our last week in style

So I've decided to shelve the 5/2 diet. First of all, it doesn't seem to suit me as I end up eating more on the days in between, as if mentally I have to "make up" for the fasting and take too literally the idea that on non-fasting days I can eat anything! I probably need to read the book. But in any case, I have devised a new weight maintenance/loss plan for being in Europe: Eat healthy when having meals at home and stay off the sweets. Eat moderately when we go out. I think the balance here for me is to take what I have learned about the fasting into my everyday mind. And keep on walking several miles a day and doing my yoga. Gotta move, gotta move.

Yesterday was blessed with spectacular weather. We had sunshine all day long. It was a day in which to renew and revive ourselves. I continue to endeavor never to take one of those for granted. We walked easily over five miles, down the country lane into the village. On the way we met Diane, a neighbor, who walked with us, and we had a very pleasant chat along the way. She showed us a different route that avoided the main street into the village and gave us more river time. Yahoo! I love finding out about new footpaths, especially ones that take us out of the flow of traffic and put us along the water. I feel like I have found out a secret that no one else knows about.

After walking round village (many of the locals don't use the word "the," nor do they use complete words. For example, "around" is just "round") and buying *The Velveteen Rabbit* for Hen for his first birthday in addition to a few other errands, we walked back along the canal to the Garden Center. This place is so cheerful with its colorful flowers outside, the beautiful displays of dried flowers and vases inside the store, and the best part: the tea shop.

When we first entered, we almost left because there were no empty tables, but as we pondered it, one opened up for us. Joe ordered a BBQ chicken sandwich on ciabatta along with a slice of—you guessed it—chocolate cake. Results will be posted shortly on the chocolate cake contest. It is part of our mission to find the best one in Uppermill.

I had the smoked salmon wrap and a slice of cheesecake, and we had a pot of tea between us. It was an absolutely posh lunch. This is when I realized that part of this adventure is about enjoying the food without guilt or remorse. Life is here to be cherished. Every bit of it.

With the sun still shining on us, we strolled along back to village, bought some veg, and met Gary at the pet store, who, as it turned out, sold cracked corn, which we needed for the chickens. Yay! We shall buy some tomorrow and taxi home. Today was just too good a day not to walk. And walk we did. Joe's bag was quite full, but he didn't let me take a turn, bless him. Uphill we went, after a pleasant walk along the canal. We were bursting with good cheer over the day, as was everyone we passed.

The part of the canal walk that runs between the edge of the village and the climb back up to the main road was where we usually meet a lot of nice dogs and watch the geese and ducks gliding around on the water. The ducks were feeling spring in the air, splashing and diving under the water. I could get used to this walk, and in fact it already is so familiar.

Back home, Joe cleaned out the chicken coop, and the girls gave us four more eggs! They hadn't been laying many eggs at all when we got here, and now they are producing. Joe says it's the increased corn he gives them and because he talks to them. I'm sure Ava and Jack will be quite pleased.

Felix left us a note about going bowling with them and some people from Isobel's work tomorrow night. Bowling in England—now there's a first. They are really kind to us, those two.

Next day the air was a bit colder on our walk into village. Again we bought a few things and then decided, since it was a right good day to have a nice hot cup of tea, that we'd try Kitty's Cafe, which we'd walked past many a time before. What a cozy, warm place we found in Kitty's! We ordered tea for two, I got a scone with jam and clotted cream, and Joe, surprisingly, a slice of chocolate cake! And the vote was in. Out of the three places, Joe liked Kitty's cake the best, while I, having sampled each, still liked Limekiln's the best. We have very different palates when it comes to chocolate.

We got our big sack of cracked corn and a small bag of oyster shells for the chickens and took a taxi home. The chickens are going to be fat cats now (no pun intended). I wouldn't be surprised if their egg production increases or at least holds steady, and at that rate, Ava and Jack will have a nice store of eggs when they get home.

That evening, on the ride to the bowling alley in Ashton, Felix and Isobel told us about the old days in Britain and how good they were. He mentioned this the other day, and so I was very intrigued now. I asked him what was different. He replied, "Everything. In the '70s and '80s, life in this country was grand. Nobody told you how to do anything, nobody was tracking you on your phone, and you could have a laugh with people. You didn't have to be politically correct and proper. You could have a right laugh about things and people had a sense of humor."

Now, he says, you get bloody told what to do about everything. Isobel said that you buy an iron, for example, and there's directions in it that say, "'Don't use on face,' as if you're going to iron your wrinkles or something!" In spite of the fact that they both felt strongly about this, they managed to make it so funny, the way they spoke about it. Felix said that even going to the pub was different. First off, the beers weren't so strong then; they were more like water and you could drink all night and not end up in the gutter. Plus you'd have long and good conversations about life. Now, he says, people just sit round and look at their phones and don't even know how to talk. In the '70s and '80s you could go anywhere, he told us, and you didn't have to worry about anything. You could do what you wanted and you felt free.

At the bowling alley, we met many of Isobel's workmates and they set us up on a lane. The camaraderie grew amongst the four of us while bowling and before long we were laughing like mad. We bowled with two other women, Kay and Shanda. We all took turns being terrible and then improved a bit. I had the low score, an 81, on the first game and in the second game Joe won with a score of 156! It was such good fun, and we each had a free beer while we played.

After our two games were finished, the organizer of the event gave out the "prizes." Best overall score for female and male and visitor. The next prize was for best overall score for a single game and it turned out to be Joe! Well, now he was right famous and he picked his prize: a box of chocolates! He must have gotten them for me:)

Lots of pictures were taken and hugs given all around. I walked up to Joe and Felix saying that we needed a red wine and chocolate night just as Felix was saying the exact same thing—how well red wine went with chocolate. So we have fixed up that we will go back to the Swan for Sunday early dinner and then come back to Ava's place (our home away from home) for a glass of wine and sharing Joe's box of chocolates. Like the taxi driver told us, "Enjoy it, as you never know what you're going to get." If you ever told me how this sit would work out, I never would have believed it. It's been a fine adventure. Sweet dreams.

FEBRUARY 25

Catching up

I'm starting yet a new weight loss plan. I'm calling it "Think yourself thin," and I may have to copyright the name and write a book about it, if it works. I've been reading a book from the library called *The Brain's Way of Healing*, and in it a doctor explains how you can reset your pain pathways in the brain with visualization techniques. I thought if one can do that, I should be able to "reset" my body by thinking it thin!

Joe and I just returned from another lovely walk, one in which I hatched out a more precise vision of The List. It's the one in which we put together "must haves" or "very important" things about a place where we would like to live. My list to date includes the following important things: Closer to sea level, of course; close to a university that offers free classes to seniors, for when I ever get to be one; a place close to or on water; decent weather for walking (as proven by this trip to England, it doesn't have to be perfect weather—just decent—not too cold or snowy); and very important to us, loads and loads of walking trails. We decided today to take a hint from the English on that and walk four to five miles every day for the rest of our lives. We have been doing pretty well with that here and are loving it.

After a light breakfast at the Limekiln this morning, Joe wanted to explore the canal in the other direction, away from the village and away from our home away from home. And off we went, the weather working in our favor—not brilliant sunshine, mind you, but not a bad sort of day overall. The canal walk took us to the village of Diggle, where we started a loop back through the village toward Uppermill.

We met up with the canal again at a spot where there were low stone cottages glued together in a row along the water. If I could buy one, that's where I'd live, which gave me the quick realization that near water is where Joe and I like best. It's so pleasant here with the quaint stone cottages and pretty gardens.

At the spot where we stepped onto the canal path, we met up with a tall man and his four-legged companion whom we'd seen further back. He too was looping back toward Uppermill, and we walked beside him the whole way. His dog, as it turned out, belonged to a neighbor and her name was Ella. She was black and white and sported a green coat properly muddied up on the belly side. She was a mix of cocker spaniel and collie. A sweet little thing, she paddled along some ways behind him and he kept saying, "She'll catch up." Big John was his name, a fit and slender man, though very tall so that it was his height that matched his name. He was 70-some years old and told us he walks 30 miles a week!

Yesterday saw us walking as well, this time with our now good friends Isobel and Felix, to the Swan in Dobcross. It was a fine, sunny day, and we enjoyed popping over the hillside with them. Conversation was easy. When we sat at the Swan, Felix wanted to know all about our lives in America, and when we started talking about the adventures that brought us here, he said, "You have a book there!" (which makes me realize that I've got a bit more writing ahead of me).

We grabbed a taxi and they stopped at our home away from home to share some of Joe's box of chocolates with us. They both hugged Joe and me warmly when they departed, and I heard Felix telling Joe, "You're a really great guy!" I really haven't seen Joe click with a buddy like that in a long while. It's a shame that they live so far apart. We promised to exchange emails, and they're going to send us pictures of Joe, who will be appearing in the next newsletter at Isobel's work for single, high-score bowler!

Joe famous in England. Who would have thought it.

FEBRUARY 27

My husband the Good Samaritan

Sometimes we learn the spiritual practices that we are seeking through life itself. Today was one such day.

Joe and I took a walk along the canal today in Uppermill, heading to our now-favorite lunch spot, the Limekiln cafe. About a block from the restaurant, along the canal, stood a woman who was collecting donations for the Canal River Trust, an organization that takes care of the canals and helps preserve them. After speaking to her for a few minutes, we left to go have our lunch. Joe offered to bring her back a cup of hot tea when we passed by after our meal, a really kind thing to do as it was a damp, cold day. And the lovely part of it was that she immediately accepted his offer, thanking us in advance.

Today, we chose to sit outside at the Limekiln to enjoy the weather, the water, and the gardens beyond. We were happy to make use of the lightweight blankets on the chairs to either sit on or otherwise wrap up in while we watch the ducks and geese play on the water.

After enjoying a delicious lunch we carried the hot cup of tea back to the woman, whose name was Claire. She was most appreciative. And as we walked away, a thought dawned on me about the perfection of the whole scene I'd just witnessed.

The true heart of compassion lies not only in performing unselfish acts of kindness, but equally in showing true compassion for the Self by being able to receive such kindnesses. It reminded me of Karuna Reiki®, which invites us to Compassionate Action, and asks us to show that same compassionate action towards ourselves.

When life offers you pleasure and teachings in the same 24 hours then that is surely a grand day.

FEBRUARY 29

Anywhere; the world

This sit has been a funny thing for me, with many mixed feelings: first with Joe being sick and the whole month stretching ahead of us, followed by a big shift with Joe's return to health and discovering the land together and meeting new friends Felix and Isobel. I've had moments of wanting to be at home and moments of wanting to stay forever in this beautiful place.

On the Sunday past, as we sat in the pub with Felix and Isobel, Felix talked about why so many people want to move to the UK, and then do, it seems, whether it be with passports and visas or without. He says, all in all, it's still a safe place to live. "No one will shoot ya, except maybe the police. The government will feed and house you and the NHS will take care of you if you are sick."

And, he repeats, it's a pretty safe place. I can hear his voice in my head, his accent from Oldham and who knows where else, what they call a "broad" English accent—not refined, as Felix will tell you. I like to listen to him and Isobel. Their voices and manner of speaking make me feel safe. There's a singsong quality to it that's soothing, even though they cut off their words and Joe or I often ask them to repeat themselves. Like when Felix kept talking about the "toorists" and how they come here without cell phones so they can't be tracked. And after the third time or so, I, in my innocence, said, "But *we're* tourists!" which brought a huge laugh, for he was, as you might have guessed, saying "terrorists," but because of that broad English accent of his, I had heard tourist. Funny that.

During this past month in Grasscroft, we began to dig into this country. I suddenly knew that we aren't like the hens out back anymore, simply scratching the surface of England. No, we'd begun to dig in and grow some roots. We aren't here to be tourists (or terrorists, for that matter!) and see the sights, although there are some beautiful sights to see. We aren't all about ourselves being caught up in our own world. We are here to live, to experience the day-to-day life, to become part of the community we are in, whether that means going bowling with new friends or bringing tea back for a stranger or walking alongside a man and his dog down the canal, sharing stories.

We got sick and went to the doctor here, and we rode in cars and buses and taxis, and we walked. And every part of this beautiful place was felt by our feet and blown through our hair; it reddened our cheeks, warmed our skin, and lit up our eyes with its beauty and quiet strength—strength in both the people and the place. We had been changed by it and wondered how we'd feel when we went home to the States. Would we miss the footpaths and the friendly people and the green?

Tomorrow we will go forward to our next sit and then the next, but we'll be different. And we'll recognize one simple fact: Joe and I can live anywhere.

Huntingdon...
a Short Break

MARCH 3

A feathered nest

I sit atop my perch in this cozy neighborhood in the town of Huntingdon, a market town in Cambridgeshire, England. My nest is painted robin's egg blue and contains a cozy bed made of white sheets and a satin cover with a quilted headboard. The walls are decorated with scenes from the sea and one of a woman in fancy dress holding an armful of white daisies. There are his and hers bathrobes at the bottom of our bed and a bag full of brochures to tell us about the town. We've landed in a very nicely feathered nest indeed.

How wonderful the ways the Divine works in bringing us exactly what we need at all times. This sit, a "fill-in" week once we decided against going to Ireland, was meant to be just a place to rest our heads before going to Scotland. We expected no more or no less. Instead, we've found everything: a cozy and immaculate home and wonderful dear people, whose essence is one of grace and kindness. We are truly, once again and always, blessed.

In numerology, we are staying in a six house this week. The six is the nurturer, and we felt very nurtured and at home here instantly, a first for me on this housesitting adventure. All of the places we've stayed have been wonderful, but there has been some kind of adjustment period at each of them, so to feel instantly at home in a place is a rare thing indeed. Our gracious hosts served us a beautiful meal with the style of a five-star French restaurant, starting with champagne with olives and nuts, followed by a baked salmon with cherry tomatoes and French-cut beans alongside cooked new potatoes, all accompanied by a white wine. For dessert, some fine cheeses and crackers along with berries and cream.

Better than the food was the company. Both James and Mia shared some of their personal history with us. James told us of a life of being raised in Zimbabwe on a 5000-acre farm owned by his mother, Oriana, and his father, Zuko. He spoke of the good years and those that followed with a political regime that forced his parents from their beloved home. We all shared our stories of parents, past and present, and bonded in a way that would be unlikely for two couples who'd just met a few hours prior.

And then there is Ella—sweet and lovely Princess Ella, one beautiful and adored cat who will share the house with us this week. Undemanding except when it comes to her food, Ella gets a few little kibbles in her bowl several times a day and otherwise adorns the house quite nicely. We are in sync with each other immediately.

This morning we woke to sweet sunshine, and I cannot wait to greet the day with my feet and my heart. It promises to be a good week, and I am rejoicing in a phrase I think epitomizes our housesitting adventure: You never know what you're going to get. It makes me realize that expectation is something that interferes with reality in some sense. It's better to jump into the unknown without any expectation. You might be pleasantly surprised.

MARCH 7

A week in Huntingdon

This is our shortest sit yet. Just 10 days and we crouch here like someone on a diving board, ready to spring into our next pool of adventure—in Edinburgh! But for the time being, we enjoy the little house in Huntingdon. I keep thinking of Ava, when she walked us to the elevator at the train station in Manchester. I hugged her and told her, "Thanks for taking such good care of us," and as we stepped onto the elevator, I looked up at her and saw tears in her eyes. A small thing, perhaps to some, but not to me. It took me by surprise and at the same time allowed me to see the inside of her just as I have been on a search for the inside of me. It made me think of that line from the movie "On Golden Pond," when Ethel, played by Katherine Hepburn, tells Billy, "Sometimes you have to look hard at a person."

I personally think you always have to look hard at a person, especially to look past the lens of judgment that we all wear. We are all judging one another in every moment, aren't we—even when we think we are being kind. We are judging what someone wears, what her shape is, how she laughs, what a person says—just absolutely everything. All along I knew that Ava was a kind person and appreciated that both she and her husband had shown us true hospitality. But in that naked moment, when the tears welled up in her eyes, I saw her right to her soul.

It is Sunday and we are in Huntingdon with our UK family, celebrating Mother's Day in England with Nikki, Al, and Henry and Nikki's parents, Ruth and Mike (Mother's Day is celebrated in March in the UK). And indeed, they are our family whilst we are here, and will always be our British family from this time forward. We went to a place called The Horseshoe restaurant in nearby St. Neots. We learned there that not all pubs are equal; some are far superior to others, like this one. Not only did they have a highchair ready for Henry, he was also supplied with plastic dishes, placemat, cup, spoon, and bib! The wait staff couldn't have been more genuine or helpful and the food was delicious.

The meat eaters (everyone except me) had the Carvery, a buffet consisting of roast pork, stuffing, veg, and the works. I ordered the veggie dish, which was a tart stuffed with spinach and artichokes and cheese. Very delicious. And we enjoyed dessert and great conversation. Henry ate more than most of us put together! Just kidding, but that boy sure can tuck into a meal. He is the happiest and most well-adjusted baby I've ever met. He winked at me as if to say, "Hey, it's been a month, but of course I remember you."

Hen will be one year old next month, and he's not gone through that shy stage that children do when they suddenly pretend not to know you and don't want to be with anyone but Mum. Not this boy. He is a social magnet, and if he could have gotten down and walked, he would have tottered over to the next table and introduced himself to the little ones there. He was fascinated by them. The best part was that in the past week, Henry has learned to point with his index finger and that's all he did when he wasn't eating his lunch. He pointed at everything, with concentration and earnest fascination. We couldn't stop giggling.

Also, Nikki said he's put together proper crawling in the past two days. I imagine by the time we see him in another month he will be running the country.

Every moment spent with Nikki and her family was lived to the fullest and still our time together went by much too quickly. Ruth brought along two sweaters that she had hand knit for Henry, complete with his name on the inside collar. She makes them all the time. They are fabulous, as is she. We decided to rendezvous in April when we return from Scotland. It is hard to believe that we are now talking about the last few days of this trip. It will be here before we know it.

The home here in Huntingdon is quite small but very comfortable. However, I am finding my allergy to cats is even more intense, though, with this lovely Princess Ella. She is the cat that everyone would love to have, or at least I would. She is always thinking of her next meal, but is ever polite about it and is just pleasant to spend time with (aside from my sneezing and coughing). I will try an antihistamine tomorrow.

This town is very walkable, and Joe loves being a "town mouse," yet we are finding some country walks to satisfy my need for open space. Yesterday we found a floodplain that used to act as a racetrack and was once an airfield. It's possible to walk the entire perimeter of this vast field in about an hour. I hope we will do it again. The man we met the first day who told us about the field also said it was the biggest wildflower plain in England in spring. I wish it were spring now. I'd love to see those wildflowers.

Stores are close by here. No more mile and a half to the grocery store, although I am missing our five-mile walks. I loved them, but my legs are appreciating a bit of a break. We walked the entire town today and it is much different here. What's most different? It's flat!

Tonight Joe popped down to the corner for takeaway fish and chips. Easy-peasy and not too much cleanup! After dinner, we find ourselves spending a quiet evening together, which has been the norm for us here in England. Tonight, Joe is on his iPad and I am typing away. It is pleasant to be together and yet taking up silence in our own ways. Tomorrow… Cambridge?

MARCH 8

King of the Belgians

Yesterday was a cloudy day to start, but became brighter with a suggestion of sun. It was cold, but I felt housebound after several days of mooching about the house with coughs and sniffles (interspersed with walks of course!). A surge of energy rushed in, along with the familiar desire to wring the sponge of the day. I spent the morning planting seeds for future Reiki classes, something I haven't felt drawn to doing before this.

There is something about this sit that suggests a turn toward the end of our stay here in the UK, and natural movement toward the future and all it will bring. The end isn't here yet, by any means, but we've definitely "crossed over" from the feeling of everything at home being so far away that it doesn't bear thinking of to thoughts of what is to come. I have asked the Divine to please help me keep it to one thought at a time, especially after this morning, when I had an anxious moment and discussed with Joe all the "things" about to change. We decided together (those are the best decisions) that we would move forward step by step, one decision at a time and Joe agreed to continue to be the rock to my leaf, giving me a firm place to rest when I am in danger of floating every which way.

So another journey making our home wherever we roam may be in the making. Certainly our trip back to Colorado will be. And there might be a future trip to discover the Pacific Northwest to see if that is where we want to lay our heads and rest our feet. Our feet seem to be on the move lately, though, and not the worse for it, although I think Joe could do with a bit more rest. In this next sit in Scotland, I will try to contain my enthusiasm for going and doing so much, and give Joe room to take his leisure time as he wishes.

We got on the bus to go over to the King of the Belgians' pub, named best pub in Cambridgeshire for 2015. This pub was established in 1541 and was said to be the favored pub of Oliver Cromwell, who lived in

Huntingdon.[14] The owners greeted us warmly, and we had something different for lunch…pizza! Gooey cheese, homemade sauce and crust—a yummy, fattening delight. We walked home to Huntingdon along the nearby Ouse River. It was such a beautiful walk past long boats and the ever-present water fowl that captivate me. Besides the lovely swans and ducks, we also saw cormorants today! Arriving home after a filling lunch, a beer, and a walk, Joe was seeking a nap on our return and I spent some hours writing, dreaming, planning, emailing, and watching a little TV. It was a good day in Huntingdon.

MARCH 9

Lunch in "Peanut Butter"

It is always fascinating to me in life how we meet people. I mentioned earlier that I'd worked with Anna Twinney, a well-known horsewoman, animal communicator, and Reiki Master. The first time I met Anna was at the Rocky Mountain Horse Expo in Denver a few years ago.

Anna is well loved by many for her amazing work, including Reiki and it was through Reiki that we got to know one another personally and became friends. So it seemed like a natural fit when, last year at the Expo, Joe and I met and hit it off grandly with her Mum named Moyra. Anna is originally from the UK and now lives in Colorado, while her Mum still lives in the UK. When I told Moyra that we planned to do some housesitting

---

14 King of the Belgians, www.kingofthebelgians.com/a-brief-history.html.

there this winter, she replied with all the class and grace we've come to know about the British. "Please do let me know when you visit. I'd love to meet you for tea," she said with all sincerity. And so we connected via email and set up a date to meet.

Now the much talked about get together with Moyra and her husband Ted was finally here. We awoke to rain and more of it. We left early for our walk to the train, deciding we'd be better off at the shopping mall walking around inside than sitting around the house. We took two umbrellas. Believe it or not, this was the first time we have used umbrellas in England!

Good thing, too. It was chucking rain all the way to the station. We got there in good time and only waited about 10 minutes for the train inside the little waiting area. There were three little girls there with their mums, singing songs in a circle with hands clasped. One of the smaller ones, about five years old with pink shoes, was clearly the ringleader of the group and directed the game they were playing with song.

Once on the train, we sat across the aisle from them, and they provided entertainment for the 15-minute ride to Peterborough Station. They kept singing "choo choo" and "all aboard," and when one of the mums asked the precocious five-year-old where they were going, she said, "Peanut Butter!" We laughed, and from that moment on, Peterborough would forever be Peanut Butter in our minds and hearts.

The shopping center, where we would meet Moyra and Ted in an hour, was a quick walk through the rain, which was fortunate since we were already down one umbrella. Joe's broke the second time he opened it. We established the exact meeting place and proceeded to walk the entire shopping center, every bit of every floor. It would be our walk today, combined with walking to and from the station.

We met up with Moyra and Ted at noon. She saw us straight away and came walking briskly over to give us a hug. There was that same feeling of instant rapport that I felt when first meeting her, as if I'd always known her. So here we were, one year later, sitting in the restaurant called "The Place to Eat" in the John Lewis department store, Peterborough (known in certain circles as Peanut Butter), England, having lunch with Moyra and Ted.

It was our first time meeting Ted, a very amiable man. We talked nonstop for two hours about Moyra's work as a pastor, about Reiki, about Anna and her family, our work, our futures, and what was important to us. I found Moyra to be an intelligent and interesting woman with whom I'd love to spend more time, while Joe had a really nice visit with Ted as well. We took pictures, and Moyra and I agreed that it was all over too quickly. We would meet again, that was for certain.

It's hard to describe what a special feeling today was. When you think of all the people in this world, the idea that you can meet someone from an ocean away and then visit her in her own country, have intimate conversation and share deep truths about life, and walk away feeling just that much more blessed than you had a few hours before is really one of the special gifts life can give us, if we are open to it.

To Peanut Butter, and to Moyra and Ted. Bless you and keep you well until we meet again.

MARCH 11

Cambridge: a college town

Riding the bus to Cambridge on our last day of this Huntingdon sit, I realized how adaptive we have become. Though this sit was the shortest of all, it took us no time to feel familiar with the area. We became very used to the walk to the town center with its cobbled streets and various shops: the fish and chip shop just a skip and a jump away from the house, the Rosamund coffee shop, where we enjoyed sandwiches *al fresco* on our first day, the charity shop where I bought two books for 2 quid each and returned them for resale by the end of week, and the Falcon, where we enjoyed tea upstairs by the bay window overlooking the town.

Then there were our walks that took us further along the River Great Ouse (as opposed to the River Little Ouse), where Joe met the man with the Tupelo honey boat, where we walked back from the King of the Belgiums, where we found the old floodplain field that we walked one day.

On our river walk, we happened upon The Old Bridge House, a beautiful hotel and restaurant with its own wine shop, where we treated ourselves to a night out on our last evening. Here, we sat in an alcove that looked out to the river and were pampered by the kind young waitstaff. In lieu of dinner, we shared a nice Malbec and a cheese plate with bread and biscuits. The portions were dainty, leaving room for sweets.

We sat leisurely for a half hour to wait for them to begin serving dessert. What a rare thing to just sit and talk without needing to give up our table, not be anyplace else—just sip our wine leisurely and bask in the beauty of doing nothing.

As we sat, we tried to remember every place we've ever gone together since 2007, the year we met. We met playing horseshoes and Joe always says we've been playing ever since. We will be together nine years this July and Joe told me the other day that if he dies tomorrow, he feels that he has lived fully, especially these last nine years.

I loved the leisurely pace of our evening together at The Old Bridge House. It reminds me of what we've been told about going to mainland Europe. People in the UK say that time slows down even more. I'd like to experience that.

Walking home at night down the now-familiar path through town felt quite different than in the daylight. It's always been interesting to me how darkness can lend an altogether different sense to a place. Next morning, after saying our goodbyes to Ella who wished us a good day, we started out in a thick fog to the bus station bound for Cambridge, riding on the top of the double-decker bus. Joe loved this. It was his first time on a double decker, and he chose the seat right in front, which he called the suicide seat because, as he says, if we crash we are done for.

The bus was traveling on a road built just for the bus. From our resting place above the driver, we could see everything, including the promise of a sun burning away the fog. It's going to be a spectacular day.

MARCH 12

Cambridge: Part Two

Exciting. Old. Very different. LOADED with history. These are some of the words and phrases that I would use to describe this town. An excitement runs through me that I haven't felt for a while.

As soon as we "landed," we were approached by a man on the street to buy punting tickets. This meant taking a punting boat (guided) down the river, which wound past most of the universities. It was a hard sell, and we politely promised to check it out. But 10 minutes later, we booked a two-hour walking tour instead.

We toured Queens College with its massive courtyard that somewhat reminded me of the open courtyard in Northampton, Massachusetts where my oldest daughter graduated from Smith College. One woman in our tour group asked how they keep the grass so green and manicured, later lamenting to me about the state of her own grass. The size of the courtyard combined with the lush green presented a beautiful picture.

A tour of King's College led to the chapel, where Joe was intrigued to learn all about the War of the Roses. War is central to this country's history, and even more so in Scotland. As the guide wove his tale, I wandered over to the stand where people light candles in the church and put in 50 pence to light one for my Mom and Dad, who have both passed on from this life. It reminded me so much of being a young girl in church with them, lighting candles after Mass and putting a few coins in the slot.

The most interesting place to me on this tour, beyond the grandness of the colleges, was a small pub called the Eagle, which was famous for two things. One was its ceiling, which was covered with the writing of WWII Royal Air Force soldiers who wrote their names, where they flew, the names of their comrades, or just about anything else. The writing remains, a testament to that time and those men. The second claim to fame was commemorated by a plaque that hung on the wall behind one of the booths in the pub. The plaque stated that, in 1953, on that very spot, Francis Crick and James Watson first announced their discovery of DNA.[15]

It was plain to see from listening to our guide, a former history professor at Cambridge, that the history of this city and the narratives it contains are endless sources of fascination and study for many. It becomes a passion that feeds them—this constant seeking of new information.

After our tour, we traced our steps backwards to the very same Eagle pub, now bursting with life, and ate lunch while sitting at a small table placed actually inside the old fireplace. The afternoon was warm and lovely, and we spent a nice evening with our homeowners, Mia and James, who'd just returned from their trip that day. We shared a supper of aubergine parmesan —which I had prepared ahead of time—and a bottle of Madeira wine, which they'd brought back with them.

Seriously lovely, gentle, and kind people are these two. The next

---

15 Ivan Noble, "'Secret of Life' Discovery Turns 50," BBC News online, February 27, 2003, www.news.bbc.co.uk/2/hi/science/nature/2804545.stm.

morning, James surprised us all by laying out a lovely breakfast of bircher, followed by a soft-boiled egg and toast. Bircher is made by soaking oatmeal in apple and hemp juice with chia seeds, flax seeds, and raisins. It is eaten cold and is very delicious! I shall make it on our next sit.

James said that to have an egg and toast on Sunday was a tradition in their family and then laughed at himself as he realized it was only Saturday! He said they would have it again tomorrow.

After breakfast, James cleaned up the kitchen while Joe and I shared a Reiki session with Mia. She was feeling the effects of her allergies more than usual. It was her first Reiki experience, and she seemed most grateful and touched by it.

She then suggested taking some pictures, and we had such fun taking selfies of the four of us in the mirror, followed by shots of just Joe and me and one with Princess Ella. They took us to the station with big hugs and fond farewells, sending us off with a box of cookies and little candies and a gift box of Madeira cake!

On the train, we sat at a table across from a woman named Kristi and her grandson, Leo. When we first sat down, I must admit to feeling slightly annoyed at sitting across from a small boy, a young man who at first didn't seem at all interested in our presence. He was oblivious, in fact.

It's hard to admit openly how mean and selfish it was to feel this way, simply because I wanted leg room and a bit of quiet. But we mustn't question the Universe in all her Divine ways. And the dark-haired, brown-eyed, six-year-old Leo definitely appeared across from me for a reason. He was traveling to Scarborough to see his Grammy Kristi's house for the first time and to meet his great-grandparents.

And, as is our way, we began to chat with our fellow travelers. They would only be on the train for the next hour, but every minute seemed an eternity to Leo, who continually asked how long it would be. Kristi welcomed the conversation and the help we became in entertaining young Leo, who was most anxious for his train ride to be over.

At one point when he became particularly restless, I suggested a game of "I'm going on a picnic and I'm taking a… ." Though only six, Leo was very bright and had an excellent memory. He smiled a lot while we played, and his anxiety was lost for a bit as he became totally immersed in the game.

A little while later, he wanted to know my name and then called me "Rose Gram" and held my hands in his little ones. All three of us "grownups" reassured, entertained, and distracted Leo on what felt like a long journey for him. "Train is slowing down, Grammy Kristi. Is this our stop? When will it go faster? Why is it stopping, Grammy?"

We played "I Spy," and Leo, as it turned out, made up his own words. He became Leo Maca and I became Rose Cam. Every time I said his "secret" name, he smiled widely. Just before their stop, he grabbed my arms, saying, "We'll be going soon."

I only spent an hour with that child, yet the feeling of him still remains in my heart. After Leo and his Grammy Kristi departed, I teetered down the aisle of the moving train to buy us some sandwiches at the train cafe. The man behind the counter seemed so steady on his feet compared to me, and when I commented on it, he said, "Walk like a penguin. If the train tilts one direction you tilt the other." Sound advice, and I found myself walking with my toes out wide on the return journey to my seat.

As I sat enjoying the rest of the train journey, watching the beautiful scenery, suddenly the ocean appeared! And I thought about little Leo and what message he might be bringing me; perhaps a message about reconnecting with kids. I thought about all the jobs I've had in the past, and the ones I liked the best were summer camp with the kids and horses and teaching at the therapeutic riding school in Malvern, Pennsylvania. It was worth some consideration for a new path or for revisiting an old one!

Scotland

MARCH 14

Edinburgh

An enchanting city. I want to spend some serious time here. What a place to write. It is a city of writers: Sir Walter Scott, Robert Louis Stevenson, Ian Rankin, J.K. Rowling, to name just a few. I can imagine studying medieval literature or the classics here, learning the history and the battles, being inspired by it all, and then going out into the wilds of Scotland to explore nature.

On our first evening in Edinburgh, we left our bed and breakfast and walked to Leslie's Bar, which was just a few blocks away, and had the best prawns I've ever tasted. They were deep fried, which I don't usually like, but the juiciness just exploded in our mouths with the sweet flavor of the prawns.

Next day we walked and walked down to the main part of town and along the Royal Mile toward Edinburgh Castle. Once there, we decided to pay our way in and take a walking tour of the castle. It was magnificent, with a guide dressed in traditional Scottish kilt and hat. He was funny and very animated, and helped us to understand the castle's history. "The castle has never been taken by force," he kept repeating, and seeing the fortress that it is today, it is easy to understand why.

They have a great cannon in the courtyard that is fired each day at 1 p.m. Our guide explained that the most likely time to shoot off the cannon would be noon, but, since the Scots are known for watching their pennies, and the number of shots of gunpowder used to fire the cannon had to match the number of hours on the clock, it was decided on 1 o'clock instead. If they fired it at noon, they would be firing it 12 times; firing it off at 1 would only require one time to signal one o'clock! Saving gunpowder means saving pennies!

Many of the buildings were open for us to tour, and we were most interested in seeing the Crown Jewels and the sandstone that is used in coronations. The actual stone is housed here in Edinburgh's castle, although when it comes time for a coronation, it is moved to London and placed inside a chair that the newly appointed King or Queen sits upon. The stone signifies the royalty's connection to the earth.

I love the Scots! They are so full of heart, their voices singing a lolling tune that is so easy on the ear. They are rich and full in and of themselves, and proud of their beautiful country.

After the tour, our guide invited us to sample Edinburgh Castle's famous whiskey, and so we had two complimentary drams. It was good, which surprised me because normally I can't even stand the smell of whiskey. We bought a bottle for Joe's cousin, who will enjoy it very much. I also bought gifts for both daughters; a small ring for my youngest, and a pair of gloves for her sister, along with a beautiful lambswool Scottish scarf for myself. Try as I might, I couldn't convince Joe to buy anything for himself (yet), but I will keep trying.

A long and beautiful day spent in the outdoors exploring Edinburgh ended that evening with a nice dinner at Salisbury Arms, which was also quite close to our B & B. Who could ask for anything more?

MARCH 15

Edinburgh: Part Two

Our second day in Edinburgh began with breakfast at the Kingsway, cooked by Gary and served by Lizzie, the owners. They are a couple in their late 30s, maybe early 40s, fit and thin, and nice as can be. Joe had the porridge and I the smoked salmon with scrambled eggs on a bagel. Delicious! We met other people from America. They were from Alabama, staying at our B & B—a shrinking Universe. We took Bus #8 to the Botanical Gardens, which were heavenly for me with beautiful grounds lush with many areas well-suited for fairies! It made me think of my friend from the U.S. who taught me about fairies. Little paths that wound up and down and around back on themselves like a beautiful fairylike maze made me feel light in my step and almost wanting to skip.

And the birds. The Scottish robin is quite different than its American brother. It is much smaller and delicately colored with a dainty orange the color of a sunset. An inky black bird with an orange beak was bathing in a small pool, and I snapped his picture. Once he realized that I'd rudely interrupted his bath, he flew to a nearby bush. Can't say I blame him. I apologized for wanting to capture his loveliness. A world of happy gardens and vast lawns sprinkled with children running here and there, heightened by a perfectly glorious and warm sun-filled day, seemed a special gift to Edinburgh's inhabitants in mid-March.

We entered one of the greenhouses filled with plants and silent steady trees that loomed high toward the greenhouse ceiling. I had to hug one, a real heartfelt hug, not unlike I would give a person. I could have stayed all day to play and to pray.

But soon we left the gardens to walk along the river to Leith, about two and a half miles. Nothing bad about that. Welcoming a rest and a drink in Leith, we took a tip from a local bartender (instead of going to the restaurant where we'd made reservations) to find ourselves at a small pub on the water, sitting outside on a dock with a cheese plate and a pint for each of us. Happy, happy, joy, joy.

We sat alone, as the other patrons apparently thought it still a bit too chilly to be dockside, but we cuddled inside our jackets and enjoyed every bite, every sip, every moment of the view together. Later we walked back to the posh restaurant to cancel our lunch reservations, thanking the young man for the tip. He winked in reply and told us to come back, anytime at all. He had known that a good thing for a lot fewer quid lay just around the corner.

We caught Bus #16 back to the famous Princes Street, where the shrine to Sir Walter Scott greeted us and Princes Park beckoned below. So many people were sitting on the benches that looked out over the skyline of the Royal Mile above. I'd say you would never tire of looking at that view, especially on a day that's been given like this one.

We walked down Princes Street in search of the Build a Bear store to purchase not a bear, but a rabbit for young Henry James' first birthday. I recorded my voice to be placed in the rabbit's paw—a reminder, I humbly hope, of me to Henry when I'm 4,000 miles away. I tried to get Joe to speak on the recording too, but he bowed out, saying it was all to be me.

Then back across the street we went, down to Princes Park and up again to curve around and head back up many steps to the Royal Mile. We arrived a bit breathless, but with our exhilaration still intact, and steps before we reached the Mile, Joe spotted the Writer's Museum! The walkways were covered with large paving stones, inscribed with famous writers' quotes, such as "Sing out the silence; fill for ever and ever the emptiness" by James Allan Ford. There were many others, and I loved looking at them and wondering about those who wrote here. The museum was closing for the day but we will return.

I am in heaven for inspiration here. My body is aching as I lay in bed, legs weary from walking, back muscles a bit sore, but my heart is very full.

MARCH 16

One more day

Leaving Edinburgh this morning on the bus to Melrose, it felt as though I was leaving behind a bit of my heart, hoping I will come back to find it again. I imagine this is the way of magical places; Paris for some, Rome for others, mountaintops or seasides for others still. For me, in this moment, it is Edinburgh. It is a place full of stories. After our first brief affair, I still find it beautiful, enchanting, some "one" I could spend a lot of time getting to know who is full of secrets waiting to be discovered.

Yesterday, the weather was much changed from that of the previous one (what a difference a day can make). We hunkered deeper into our coats for our walk up and down and back up the Royal Mile, looking to buy or exchange a few small gifts we'd bought, grabbing any opportunity to duck in out of the cold grey mist to shop, converse with proprietors (mostly Joe), or have a cuppa (mostly me).

As per usual, especially due to the conversational attitude of my traveling companion, we had good chats with the man outside the fudge shop, who gave us free samples along with directions (we bought a wedge of the chocolate mint for future snacking), the woman at the small souvenir shop who was on her way to France to meet a friend, a man selling music and eight-inch guitars in the indoor market, and a ticket taker at Holyrood Palace. Holyrood Palace is one of the places the Queen stays when she is in Scotland; it sits at the bottom of the Royal Mile, while Edinburgh Castle occupies the top end.

We took an audio tour of the Palace and I found myself looking longingly out over Holyrood Park, but today was not the day to wander the hills, so we hopped the #35 bus to St. Mary's Street, where we climbed the hill over to Dalkeith to catch the #3 to Mayfield Street.

But here is where our day took an unexpected turn (the ones I like the most). Enchanted by a billboard showing *Mary Poppins* at the Festival Theatre, I tugged at Joe's sleeve hard enough to make him cross the busy street with me and pop inside. (He knows me well enough by now to know that when I'm on the scent of something it's futile to try and stop me.)

Inside the theater a friendly ticket salesman talked with us at length about the premier of the show that night, *Tom – A Story of Tom Jones – the Musical*. Tickets were 25–40 quid each. Since this was our last night in the city, I hoped to nudge Joe into it, but he didn't seem very enthusiastic until the man offered us free tickets. Sold! To the red-headed woman and the man with the white hair!

We've become more proficient at getting the bus and so we took the #3 into town at 6 p.m. to have a bite to eat in the theater's cafe prior to the show. Nice food. I had a chestnut, mushroom, and kale tart with a beetroot and goat cheese salad, and Joe enjoyed a three-cheese grilled sandwich with tomato-basil soup, all for 20 quid. The show was fun and lively and filled with people upwards of 60, I'd say. No doubt they were longtime Tom Jones fans. The man to my right at the end of the aisle, who walked with a cane and seemed a bit distant at first, was soon tapping his feet and nodding his head to the music along with everyone else. The women in the audience were especially enthused when the actor, who played Tom, performed some of his most popular songs, especially his biggest hit, "It's Not Unusual." He was a fantastic singer, possibly better than Tom himself. (Sorry, Tom, if you're reading this. No offence intended.)

It re-awakened in me another aspect of myself. I could really enjoy going to the theater from time to time! I shall look for small venues in and around St. Boswell. As my sister told me, any theater production in the UK will be worth seeing as all the actors are all classically trained. Who knows? Maybe we'll take the train up to see a matinee in Edinburgh. Either way, I'll always have Tom to remember!

MARCH 17

Happy St. Pappy's Day!

In my family, we always call St. Patrick's Day "St. Pappy's Day" after my Dad, an Irishman who loved to celebrate it. Since he worked in an auto body shop, he could always spray-paint his work shoes green for the occasion and that was only one of many other fun traditions. For my brother, my sisters, and me, it will always be St. Pappy's Day on March 17th.

It's hard to believe that we have been in the UK for almost four months now, and still have a month to go. In some ways it seems an eternity and in others, a blink.

After a magical three days in Edinburgh, we took our last National Express bus to Melrose, in the Scottish Borders, to meet our newest homeowner, Harriet, and her sister Lily. The Scottish Borders is an area south and east of Edinburgh that consists of several counties and villages in southeastern Scotland. In the center of the Borders lies the village of St. Boswell. This was to be our temporary home for the next month.

We packed Harriet's Mini full between all of our bags and the four of us, and headed for a whirlwind tour of the area. It is always interesting and also taxing on the brain to try to assimilate all the information so helpfully given by the homeowners. It is an Evelyn Wood speed reading version of house, pets, surrounding areas, everything you should see and do, and all else packed into a few short hours.

To add to that excitement is the stimulus of being with and getting to know new people for the first time, usually over dinner, drinks, and dessert, while fighting the yawns from a busy day of travel. Landing in a new place always throws off the body barometer for some reason. It takes time to adjust to the energy of a new place. Reiki helps.

The house for this sit is beautiful and the cats, Hero and Daisy, are a most unusual breed. They're Ragdoll cats, which means that their hair is very long, and they are rather exotic looking. They eat prawns for breakfast every day, and generally, as has been the case with all the cats where we have stayed, are King and Queen of the household. I don't know if that's the general rule for all cat owners, but it certainly seems true for the people who have cats here in Britain. Hero and Daisy have a measuring cup that sits in the bathtub, which is where they best like to drink, although Harriet said they would prefer it if you would turn on the tap for them and let them drink that way. So far we have seen them only periodically, as they haven't decided who we are and what the heck we are doing staying with them.

Before they left the next morning, Harriet gave Joe and me a gift: our own mugs and the keys to drive her Mini, the car she says is her baby. No pressure there. They left some food for us to finish up, enough so that I could avoid driving The Baby for at least the first day. The "real" grocery stores were eight-plus miles away, down the A68 in Galashiels, and, even though I've seen the town, I couldn't find it with a magnifying glass and a GPS, neither of which I happen to have.

So this first morning after they left for their trip, Joe and I decided to explore on foot, the way we best like to see the world. We agreed that we would just take it easy, as the day before I was strangely tired and unable to focus. But the sun was beckoning, and so we began by walking just to the road where the pub was to see if we could get any sort of clue which way Galashiels was, for future reference. Of course, once we got there, I asked Joe if he wanted to walk to the Garden Center, about three-quarters of a mile down the road. He hadn't noticed it the day before when we explored the town with Harriet and her husband Bob (but I had!).

This Garden Center was called the Milestone Garden and Leisure

Center. Walking to garden centers and resting at our leisure was certainly a fun pastime of ours on this journey. These delightful places, the garden centers of England, are so beautiful and always have a restaurant that usually serves full afternoon tea. It is such a surprise and delight to find them, as we don't have anything like it in the US. The day was spectacular and getting better every minute when I spied two donkeys. I'd forgotten about the donkey sanctuary that Harriet told me about the day before. Detouring into the path that led to the sanctuary, we petted and offered Reiki to the many donkeys in the field, some of whom were quite curious about us (or what we might have had to eat). So cute! So yes, not quite horses, but adorable all the same. We walked back to the barns and asked the woman outside if we could set up a time to offer formal Reiki sessions to the donkeys! She took our information and promised to pass along the request to the manager. Fingers crossed. This could be a great gig. (Unfortunately, it never did pan out.)

Reiki shared with animals is a whole other story. Most animals love Reiki and are here to teach us many things about energy and even more so about unconditional love.

We crossed the road then to the Garden Center, where we decided to have lunch on the back patio, with the sun on our faces. Warmth, sunshine, and sandwiches. For us, it was heaven on a deck. After a while, another man came out to share the sun, and Joe struck up quite a conversation while I basked in the perfectness of the afternoon, sun so hot on my face I thought I might get a Scottish sunburn!

The man, named Ralph, shared with us another way to walk back to St. Boswell besides the busy road. A footpath ran along the donkey sanctuary that led to a walk along the river. Of course there would be a footpath! This is the UK. There's always a footpath. Love this country.

We walked alongside the river Tweed and every step was magnificent, even though we were never sure if we were going the right way. A couple of times, the path branched off and Joe would take one branch and I another, meeting back at our break-off point for consultation, but always deciding to stay along the river. Then it happened.

I was taking a picture of the river downstream when Joe took my arm. "Rose, look! Look now!" he whispered urgently. I turned my head to see something dark flash under the water. "It's an otter!" he said. We watched. It came up again. We walked cautiously backwards to get a little closer and the otter came up just on the other side of some brush, not 50 feet from where we stood. He looked straight at us, smelling us, and retreated back under the water. We continued walking up a hilly path along the river's edge and turned back, only to see him one more time. We were both supercharged after that, and could have walked miles with the adrenaline of seeing that otter. Otter medicine means woman energy. Time to play.

Little did we know it at the time, but we had discovered the magic and wonder of St. Cuthbert's Way. St. Cuthbert was a saint who lived from 635–687 A.D. and the way is 62.5 miles long across the Scottish borders and out to the Northumberland Coast.[16] The walk follows in St. Cuthbert's footsteps, and, for the next month, so would we. We were to feel the magic of this sacred footpath, time and time again, as we walked it in every kind of weather. Each day, on the walk, Joe found small, white feathers. We

---

16 "St. Cuthbert's Way," Scotland Great Trails, www.stcuthbertsway.net/index.html.

learned later they were messages from the Angels.

MARCH 19

Driving Miss Mini

Our second day in the Scottish Borders loomed cloudy and rather cold. After a sluggish morning in which we slept late, due to a seminar that kept us up till 2 a.m., I decided that I "needed" tea bags, as I had no more black decaf tea, my signature beverage.

As Joe slept in, I mapped out our journey, already feeling nervous in the pit of my stomach about driving Miss Mini. She is a beautiful Mini Cooper (the big kind with four doors) with just 12,000 miles on her—a six speed and of course here in Scotland, you shift with the left hand, mind you. For those of you unfamiliar with driving in the UK, it is, indeed, that you sit on right side of car, drive on left side of road, shift with left hand (I still find myself automatically leaving out the word 'the' in my sentences as the Scots often do). Which means that when you turn right you cross over the traffic, feeling all the while that you must for some reason look backward even though you don't need to. The left turns are easy peasy; just stay in same lane.

The roundabouts are then again the most challenging of all. You enter on left, yielding right and try to figure out whether to stay on inside lane or outside lane. I prefer the ones where you stay inside. Joe and I made an agreement before heading out to Galashiels, the town where the Tesco and Marks and Spencer stores are located. Marks and Spencer is a fancy grocery store, rather like Whole Foods in the US. Joe agreed to speak only with praise for my driving, and also to help read the signs, saying "turn here" or "stay in this lane." No comments on my driving or trying to "help." This was an agreement we made back in Colyton (which I only followed part of the time).

Reiki, Reiki, Reiki to our journey. It was by then early Friday afternoon and the traffic was pretty solid going down the A68. The driving wasn't bad at all, though, and I was learning the gears, although it required me to think first about where I was shifting. Six speed with the left hand for me does not come automatically, because the gears are closer together than the five speed I drive at home, plus I am shifting with my right hand at home. I am convinced that my right brain (controlling my left hand) is slower than my left! But all's good and Joe is flowing with praise all the way.

I felt my neck muscles tighten as we approached Galashiels and had to go through more roundabouts, more turns, and more cars, but Joe said I was doing superbly and we arrived safely at the Tesco. Whew! We shopped at Holland and Barrett, my now-favorite health food store, for some organic goodies, then M&S, where you can get lovely pre-made dinners (thought we'd give them a try for fun), and our fallback for all else, the Tesco, which was extra-large and even more confusing to get into. We rode an escalator (minus stairs) down with shopping cart to exit the store. Weird! Next came the drive home, which actually went really well, except that once I got home, I felt a bit like Cameron Diaz in "The Holiday." I needed a drink!

The next morning as Joe was taking his "electric" shower in the bathroom where the hot water worked on an electrical switch, the water shut off, so it sent us on a mission to contact someone who could do something about getting things working again—i.e. the Internet, the landline, and some of the lights. He tried to reset the breaker box, but being in a different country meant everything looked different and he couldn't quite work it out. So we walked to village and from the red phone box we called Lily, Harriet's sister (I haven't used a phone box in years!) and left her a voicemail.

We then continued on to the Mainstream Trading Company, a bookstore and coffee shop to have tea and a scone and email our homeowner about the electric, where we purchased a nice bar of patchouli soap for me and a box of decaf black tea leaves for an exorbitant 6 quid, 30 pence. It turned out that all the shopping we'd done previously that day spurred on a need for tea, and tea was the one thing I'd forgotten to buy in Galashiels. But one cannot be without tea in England.

When we returned to the house, a car sat in front, and it turned out to be Harriet's Dad, who was trying to figure out the electrical problem. Between him and Joe, they located the fuse box and within seconds all was corrected. After the excitement was over, I proceeded to begin making tea, only to find no tea bowl strainer for loose leaf tea. The Universe was playing a cosmic tea joke on me, and all I could do was laugh.

We decided to walk in a different direction away from the housing development today toward the fields in back and were rewarded with a multitude of unexplored footpaths! There were beautiful winding paths through woods and along the river in both directions with an abundance of wet spring grass along the banks. I don't know what this type of grass is, but it was the lushest I've ever seen and it made the forest come alive, even though the trees were still bare. There was so much unbelievable color, even in winter. And hints of spring were indeed everywhere, with loads of flowering snowdrops all around and some flowering trees in the village.

We walked with the abandonment of youth, not caring where we were headed or for how long. The sun decided to shine on us and indeed, we could ask for nothing more than that. A good day? I'd have to say a great one.

MARCH 25

Berwick—Upon-Tweed

Good Friday. The thing I remember most about Good Friday is being a young girl growing up in a Catholic household and every year, on Good Friday, besides going to church, of course, was that my mom made us honor complete silence from noon to 3 p.m. to honor Christ's death on the cross. Let me tell you, with all due respect to Jesus, that I hated Good Friday.

For a child who could never shut up, being completely silent for three hours was just about the worst punishment in the world. The silence was absolutely endless! Did it make me a better person? I seriously doubt it. Did it make me talk any less? Definitely not. But that's what I remember every Good Friday, even now, decades later.

Since such restrictions were lifted from me years ago, when I removed myself from the dogma of religion altogether, I jumped into this day with gladness and a lightness of spirit. Today, friends, I've awoken with a joy to the world. The sun is shining and I feel well. "Let's celebrate," I said to Joe. "Let's go to the seaside."

Asking Joe to go to anyplace that's near the water is like asking a fish if he wants to get off the hook and back into the river. He's squirming already. The bus would be leaving at 9:35 to take us to Berwick-Upon-Tweed. As we waited at the bus stop, we met a lovely elderly woman named Kathleen, an Irish lass who'd moved to Scotland when she was just 18. Her parents both died tragically young and Kathleen didn't want to be taken care of by her relatives and end up with a dozen children, she said. I guessed that she meant if she stayed in Ireland, it would be the way of things that she would inevitably marry and have a lot of children. So she moved to Scotland to make an independent life for herself and has never looked back.

She ran antique stores for years and is now retired and living in St. Boswell. When I introduced myself, she held my hand and said, "Rose. I have a relative named Rose back in western Ireland. She's the only one who writes me with the news." I found myself wishing she would be riding our bus so she could tell me stories of Ireland, but it turned out that she was going on a different bus that day.

The ride to the sea town of Berwick was spectacular—wide vast fields of green, rolling hills and barely a house anywhere. This country has lots of open spaces, and unlike the American West where we live, is blessed with fertile land and fields, beautiful flowers and trees. We drove past Floors Castle near Kelso, where Joe suggested that we have a lunch one day. How fun it would be to have lunch in a castle.

Berwick is a medieval sea town that is surrounded by great walls laid in 1296. The town sits just two and a half miles from the Scottish border and has changed hands, from English to Scottish, at least 13 times in its history.[17] The River Tweed runs alongside it, emptying into the North Sea. The sea was our first desire. We asked our feet to take us there, please, past the big stone walls, along the houses fronting the water, and out on a peninsula leading to the lighthouse. The further we walked out, the stronger the wind played with us. Exhilarated by our favorite place, the seaside, and Joe's love of lighthouses, we walked to where the lighthouse stood and spent some time gazing out into the water. The sun was making brilliant patterns on the waves and a man with whom Joe struck up a conversation told us that he comes out to see seals and dolphins. Today he has seen a seal, but as long as I looked, I didn't see one.

Heading back into the village, our game now was to find the eating place that the man recommended. His directions were to "go toward those houses, through the archway, down to the left, then to the right, and it's on the left. No, I don't know the name of the place or the street name, but just go through the archway."

Solving a mystery is what I love. There are plenty of eating places and it doesn't matter where we go, but I loved the idea of trying to find the place he described. After patiently circling around with me for about 20 minutes, Joe suggested that we eat at the cafe we saw earlier on. It was called the Queen's Head Hotel, and we sat at a table for two by the window. We'd

---

17 Katie Dawson, May 1, 2010,
www.news.bbc.co.uk/2/hi/uk_news/politics/election_2010/england/8640148.stm.

started by sitting at an outdoor table until the sun hid behind some pesky clouds. The place was booming with business. It was Good Friday afternoon, between 12 and 3 and no one was practicing silence.

We ordered a delicious lunch. Joe had the lasagna, which was made quite differently than his Mom's. It was cooked with shredded meat and the noodles looked very delicate compared to our American lasagna noodles. The cheese also looked light, and it was served with a slice of the most scrumptious, warm herbed bread, whose every molecule was soaked with butter. Joe kept giving me little bits of it to taste.

I hadn't been eating much since I've been feeling under the weather these last few days and thought I should just order soup and bread. But previously, whilst sitting in the bar waiting for our table, a couple across from us made a recommendation. I wanted some fish and the waiter suggested the kedgeree. The man sitting across from us also highly recommended it, so I thought, why not? When in Rome and all that. Kedgeree is a dish made up of cooked, flaked fish, in this case it was smoked salmon and haddock with rice, egg, and spices. It was superb.

Joe's lasagna had been part of a two-course special, which is often done here. It's called a set meal, and you can order either two or three courses at a set price and then you have a certain menu to choose from. Joe's second course was dessert, and he ordered a banana split!

We sat there for a long time, both of us feeling nappish. After our windy walk and great lunch we were ready for the bus! But first we walked along the river and up to the castle walkway near the Tweed. Then to the bus stop to catch our ride back to St. Boswell. A happy day, indeed. Full of the sea and her counterpart, the Tweed, we both expressed gratitude for our many blessings, including each other.

MARCH 26

Everybody needs a Joe

Have I said this before? When traveling, you need a Joe. Not my Joe; he's otherwise occupied leaning up against me in life (unless I'm the one doing the leaning). But you just need a Joe.

Today started off slowly as the day dawned cloudy and misting rain. Around 9ish, we wandered into St. Boswell. As the rain gently doused us with moisture, we discussed the fact that we do have a car on this sit and could have driven to the village. But after these long months of getting everywhere mostly by foot, it didn't occur to either of us to do so. Besides, it probably would take longer to drive in and park than it would to walk.

When we entered the Mainstreet Trading Company, all three of the people behind the counter looked at us as though we had three heads or had sprouted great white wings (how fun would that be!). In fact, they were just waiting for the day to start. This beautiful little coffee shop and bookstore (need I say more?) offers a nice atmosphere, though it has always been very busy when we've come in before. Not today. We were the first customers. We even beat the scones out of the oven, much to my disappointment. That was to be my breakfast.

Instead Joe and I ordered a cup layered with yogurt and fruit compote and topped with their homemade granola with a pot of tea, of course, and then settled in on the comfy leather couch and chair by the bay window, no doubt a favorite spot for many. As it was Easter Saturday, one of the cakes in the display case was a fruit-filled Easter cake. Little mounds of marzipan lined its perimeter, representing the Twelve Apostles.

What a nice way to cultivate the art of doing nothing (and do it well). For those of you reading this and thinking that we are lazy bums lacking ambition, I'd say it all depends upon your perspective. The art of doing nothing is just that, an art. It takes practice and a certain amount of inner serenity, which can be years in the making.

The scones came out of the oven at 10, and I asked Joe to get me one to go. In the meanwhile, the little café was filling up with patrons. Joe became engaged in conversation with a young mom with a beautiful red ponytail. I could hear him describing our adventure here and the housesitting we were doing to her and the young man behind the counter. The young man was visiting America this summer as a camp counselor north of Scranton, not far from where I spent five summers at camp as a program director. It's always a joy to find common ground, especially when traveling.

Once Joe decided on his treat of the day to take home, which turned out to be the chocolate donut cake, and sat down beside me, the couple who sat facing away from us turned around and struck up a conversation.

The man, whose name was David, apologized for eavesdropping on Joe's conversation at the counter, and then shared with us about one of the most memorable years they'd ever had. He'd participated in a teacher exchange program, teaching high school in a place called Greenville, about 80 miles from Pittsburgh. That was in the '70s.

Not for the first time on our journey, we were reminded by people from the UK what a vast and varied country we live in, and how magnificent it is. It is nice to be shown that by looking through the eyes of someone living outside our great country. That summer, after his teaching stint, David and his wife Liz traveled the US with their small children in tow, camping here and there, going all the way west, then northward to Canada and back. David said they hadn't two nickels to rub together then, and so they camped and traveled with very little money with the help of a car they rented for next to nothing.

When they moved back to Scotland, he quit his job, and they moved down to the Borders, settling in the small village of Yetholm, where they've been ever since. They invited us to come and visit them, not just in a polite way, but sincerely over and over. Liz told us that most tourists will never visit Yetholm, and yet it is a fascinating place. I learned that the Yetholm Gypsies, whose descendants still live there, have made the village famous. Liz and David spoke of the Gypsy language that is still spoken there. We are excited to embark on a new adventure making new friends and getting to know the land of the Gypsies.

I guess you may still be wondering why everyone needs a Joe. Because, as I sat there, quietly sipping my tea and looking out the window, Joe was busy talking to people, as usual, and opening doors for us to yet another new world of experience.

MARCH 29

Two weeks in Scotland

It's hard to believe that we are now looking at just two weeks and a few days left until we leave Scotland. It feels in many ways as though we haven't had much time here in this country, and, should we come back, I'd like to spend a lot more time exploring Scotland. England is indeed beautiful and very diverse, but I sense an openness and a wildness to Scotland. Joe and I talked today about flying into Edinburgh and renting a car and heading north if we come back.

I woke up this morning with a busy mind, wondering about family members and friends who are facing challenges right now, some more than others. I thought of our lives and the changes that lie ahead for us. And while I was thinking and feeling concerned about some of those things, I was also giving myself Reiki at the same time.

Suddenly a thought came in front of all the rest. It was more than a thought; it was almost an inner request. I said to my mind, as it were, "What if I took all these worries and handed them over to you, God. What if I just let go of all my concerns about others and my unknowingness about the future and gave it all to you? Where does that leave me?" Simply spoken, it leaves me in a place of peace and childlike trust.

This certainly isn't an entirely new concept. But what was new for me was that I could almost physically see myself handing over my worries to God. Let go. Let God. How often we've heard those words, but do we really know what it means to do so? Life is life and challenges will always appear, but at the same time, if we let God handle our most challenging moments, we will begin to learn the peace of true surrender.

With Reiki, I've discovered how to have a sense of safety at all times, as though everything is already being taken care of. Reiki brings with it an innate guidance and trust in life in general. It doesn't mean I don't ever get scared. It just means that when that happens, all I have to do is remind myself to use my Reiki and know that I am always safe, always protected. That may seem like a tall order but it is one that Reiki can fulfill. It has to do with the frequency at which we hold ourselves with Reiki. We react to situations differently, seeing the more loving side of things, looking for the good in all situations, knowing that everything is already perfect. It is truly a magnificent gift given to us by Reiki, if we choose to invite it into our lives.

My walk of the day before (while Joe was napping) was through a forest of perfectly spaced trees, and the sight of them made me so happy that I hugged a number of them. When I would turn to look at yet another tree, it seemed to say, "Me next," and so I would give it a hug and move on to the next one. I could have hugged the entire forest, but then some people came and it sort of ruined my tree hugging festival. I love walking with Joe, but when I have those rare walks alone, I feel as though I'm really communing with nature. I breathe when she does; I feel the ground both cradling me and lifting my spirit up at the same time. A new walk, like the one yesterday, is especially joy-filled. And for that time I was alone with my God, in my beloved woods.

Today was a different day and I had the pleasure of sharing my walking spot with Joe. I took his hand in mine and we traveled through the forest of trees leading to the river at the magnificent spot I'd found the day before. There was a wooden desk and a chair that looked out onto the river and the fields beyond. It looked like a writing spot made just for me by Mother Nature.

This time we were joined partway by a man and his two dogs, one a black and white collie and the other a little white scruffy fur ball. There was another man fly fishing in the river. He said he didn't expect to see any fish since it was his first day out.

We left there to walk home and take Miss Mini out to the Garden Center. It was a successful journey, even though my navigator and I are still working out our communication while in route. I am feeling more confident about the little car and especially the shifting, but I still do not want to drive into any heavily trafficked areas. Today was another practice session and worth it as we thoroughly enjoyed a nice lunch of salmon cakes with dill and parsley dressing and a beautiful salad of butter crunch, watercress, colorful peppers, and a few roasted potatoes. Joe and I shared the lunch plate, and then he finished it off with carrot cake (I ate a little of the icing). We walked into Newtown, which is St. Boswell's neighboring town. It is a funny town in that all the streets are up and down a hill. We wandered there a bit and then drove back home. Our new friends who live in the Gypsy village, David and Liz, have invited us to come over tomorrow. Get ready for the ride, Miss Mini (and so will I). This will be our longest trek yet!

MARCH 30

A house sitter's heartbreak

In our search for the security of sameness, we wake up each day with an expectation of everything being exactly the way it was the day before. March 30th was such a day. For all intents and purposes, it seemed like a normal day. I was tired and still feeling the effects of being ill on this sit, but beginning the day per usual by putting out prawns for Hero and Daisy and giving them fresh water.

But Hero didn't show up for his prawns. At the time it was just a niggle of a feeling I chose to ignore, a little voice that I shushed. Yet it was unusual, because although he tends to be out carousing all night long, he usually makes an appearance in the mornings—for a yawn, for a couple of vocal hellos, for a scratch, sometimes for a prawn or two—and then off he goes to his independent boy stuff. But today there was no sign of him. Joe and I both noticed it, and he said, "Oh he's probably still out prowling. He'll be back later. You know how he is." I ignored the little voice inside and went about the day.

We spent most of the day outside, per usual, and when we came home to rest, our legs weary from walking, we did just that. We rested. After a bit, the doorbell rang and from that moment on, this day was no longer anything like the one before.

At the door was a young woman dressed in green scrubs who announced that she worked for the veterinary clinic nearby. She told us that Hero was found dead in a neighbor's yard down the road. We were shocked, to say the least. Dead? That wasn't right, I thought. How could that be?

These two kitties, Hero and Daisy, are outside cats whenever they please. They have a cat door and they can come and go as they like. Usually at night, Hero likes to be out. Daisy does too but seems to stick closer to home. I have looked out our bedroom window and have seen Hero parading down the street like he owns the universe.

We decided, after the initial shock wore off, to call Lily, our homeowner's sister. She was so empathetic and kept telling us not to blame ourselves. It wasn't our fault, Lily said over and over on the phone. It was a chance that you took whenever you let cats be in or out as they please. And true to the nature of these Scots, Hero, until yesterday, was free to roam just like us. Free to be outside or inside. Free to have a cuddle on the couch or prowl through the neighboring fields if he chose. And free to leave this world, too.

The overwhelming sense I have been struggling with is guilt. Yes, indeed. Truckloads of it. How could it have happened on my watch? Obviously I wasn't watching closely enough. Shouldn't I have known when I didn't see Hero at breakfast that he was lying (probably already dead) in the neighbor's yard down the street? Shouldn't I have assumed the worst instead of just thinking, "Oh, that Hero! He must be busy out doing his thing"? I am the house and pet sitter, after all. Aren't I supposed to be in charge of that stuff?

What if he felt neglected because we closed our bedroom door at night due to my allergies? Maybe that's why he stayed out all night. But no, that wasn't it. His owner told me he does that anyhow. He just loved being out at night. And Joe said he was indeed an independent cat. As if "independent" and "cat" need to be two separate words.

So what was this beating up of myself that was happening? I feel such sadness for the woman who will come home to one cat instead of two, one of her babies gone. It's been decided by Lily that she will tell her when she comes home and not ruin her vacation. So now we get to pretend for two weeks in our emails that all is fine. A small price really, to give her a nice holiday. There's nothing that will change things now.

On the up side of things, Daisy is now the queen of her castle and seems to love it, actually. And Hero is obviously fine with it. He is in cat heaven doing exactly whatever he likes (which he did here as well, come to think of it).

But my knowing friend Nikki suggested that I should meditate on why I was blaming myself so heavily for this occurrence. And I feel it has to do with the many, many ways we try to be in control of everything in our lives and with the fear of being in the wrong, of doing something wrong, of failing.

You see this happening to people all the time when someone dies or something tragic happens. Oh, but I wish I would have said this or that to her, or I would have done this or that and it might have changed things. Yet right now is the moment that we get to make perfect, and if we are busy trying to right yesterday's wrongs or worrying about what hasn't happened yet then we are not paying attention to the now moment. I had a niggle of a feeling yesterday and I didn't follow it. That feeling that I ignored, while accurate, would not have changed the outcome, yet if I fault myself for not being present in that moment, then again I am missing the beauty of what's happening right now.

This moment becomes instead a Divine reminder to just be with what is. And right now my heart IS full, with love for Hero, for Daisy, for Joe, for our homeowners, for my family and friends back home, for Reiki, for myself, and the Divine that flows through me—to lessons learned and carried forward. It all comes back to the Reiki Precepts[18] of *Just for Today, do not worry, do not anger.* Anger is of the past, whether it is anger against oneself or others for something. Worry is of the future—worrying about something that might happen, but in actuality, hasn't happened. But now, in the present, if we could allow our minds to be just here, just now, nothing is wrong. Everything is being taken care of. Everything is already all right.

MARCH 31

The road to recovery

No matter what the loss or grief may be, there are those stages that one must go through, albeit quickly or slowly. I don't know if I recognized all five stages exactly, but I was aware that I was phasing through something. Joe commented to me the night before that he hated seeing me

---

18 Stiene, The Inner Heart of Reiki.

blaming myself and being upset, to which I replied, "I have to move through this at my own pace." He understood, as he always does.

Joe is much more philosophical about events and less emotive than I am. I think he is better able to step out of the way and observe, certain of the grace that comes from knowing the things we cannot change.

On the day after we found out about Hero, we took ourselves for a "wee" walk in the morning. Lily and George were meant to come over after they went to the vet's office to sort out about Hero, but we weren't sure what time they would arrive. When we went to the post office, Janette, the woman who works there, told us about a luncheon they were serving in the Public Hall in the village. It was £2.50 and included homemade soup, scones, bread, cake, and tea. It was mostly for senior citizens but was open to all. By the way, if you want to know anything about anything in the village, ask Janette in the post office. She will have the lowdown.

We decided to go to the luncheon. I was feeling restless and didn't want to sit around waiting for Lily and George, so we left them a note, hoping they'd be there when we got back.

The luncheon was fun, and we found a table filled with people new to us: Jenny and her son, Ian and his wife Gillian, and a young woman from Australia who'd come to have lunch with all of them. One of the women at the next table, Marie (pronounced MAH-ree) strongly encouraged us to come to the Friday lunch being served at the church hall. Several others chimed in. We were officially part of the community.

When we arrived home, there was a lovely note and a bunch of fresh flowers from Lily and George. When I called her, Lily said that the flowers were to cheer us up and please, please don't blame ourselves about Hero.

What a completely kind gesture. Harriet's family members are really great people.

I was beginning to process his death, but every time I look down the street from our bedroom window, I imagine his soft little body lying alongside the road. Stages of grief.

APRIL 1

Getting some perspective

I have always found that death brings so much grace into our lives. It seems to bring us closer to our emotions in a way that we normally can't access. It is a time full of sad things and also joyful ones, and all are strikingly felt. Hero's passing and the beauty that arose in accepting it and moving forward is a perfect example.

It started when we stopped by the vet's office after breakfast. We both wanted to hear with our own ears what they thought about Hero's death.

Amy, the vet tech, confirmed that he was found by the side of the road and that it looked very likely that he'd been hit by a car, even though there were no obvious signs of injury. She said a simple blow to the head could have caused it, which relieved our concern about him being poisoned or something else.

Joe felt much better after that, but my shift in perspective came when I read an email from a dear friend from Scotland. She said that she has experienced and also heard about how often it happens that an animal decides to "leave" when the owners are away.

Thinking about it in this way, that we may have been put here for a higher purpose, the purpose of allowing Hero the space to leave of his own accord, left me with a different sense of it altogether. It was a reminder to me that this was not happening just to me as nothing happens just to me. Hero had his own ideas, his own free will, and was living out his life and his death in his own way.

I used to believe in accidents but I no longer do these days. And if Hero felt it was his time to go, he brought forward the circumstances under which he could leave.

In a similar situation right now is Joe's dad in Pennsylvania, miles and miles away. When we left for our trip, both he and his wife were doing okay. Since then, they have been moved to a nursing home and now Joe's dad has declined rapidly to the point of being on hospice care. The nurse we spoke to this evening said he only had days to live. But then we spoke to Joe's brother, who said the nurses don't know everything, and his Dad had recently eaten half a peanut butter sandwich. Does he want to go? As another of Joe's relatives pointed out, you couldn't really blame him if he did. This was the man who always said he was going to live to be 100 years old, who walked three miles every day, now trapped inside a nursing home without his daily walks, without his favorite foods, and minus the independence he has known for the past 86 years. What has happened to his choices?

Of course the day moved forward, despite Hero's being gone and Joe's dad being halfway between life and death. For the rest of us, at least for now, life moves on.

And a brilliant day it was. One of the warmest and brightest days we've seen in the past four months in the UK. And how did we choose to spend it? You guessed it—walking by the River Tweed.

This day we decided to drive Miss Mini down to the chain link bridge near the donkey sanctuary, about a mile and a half from our house, and park along the road where other walkers like ourselves park. We crossed the shaky suspension bridge, as I call it, Joe shaking it more since he knows I don't like it. We were finally going to explore the other side, where we've seen other people walking every time we walked the Tweed.

We found a beautiful old hotel along the river named Dryburgh Abbey. Their menu looked nice and about average cost so we will probably try to take our friend Amy there for lunch when she visits next weekend.

Once at the riverbank, we followed a footpath along the river with the sunlight glinting off the water. It was so warm we took off our coats. There is nothing that makes you feel more alive than the combination of sun, water flowing, and spring flowers coming up after a long damp winter. We reveled in it.

We came to a sign that said "Private" and Joe suggested climbing the fence, saying, "It's Scotland, we're free to roam." And roam we continued to do until we came upon a group of houses and people and a dog running towards us, along with another sign saying "Private." This time Joe didn't argue, but agreed to turn around after petting the dog.

Every moment of the walk back was just as delightful, and we ended the day by visiting our new friends Eloise and Arthur. They are in their 80s and are the parents of our homeowners. We invited them to join us for the community lunch at the church tomorrow. They gave us a tour of their little cottage. When I commented to Eloise about the TV in their bedroom, she leaned over to me and said in a conspiratorial whisper, "I love cowboys!" She pointed below her TV, where she had cowboy movies stacked up.

On our walk to lunch the next day, Eloise held my arm firmly to steady her gait, and we talked of our children. The lunch at the church hall consisted of butternut squash or split pea soup, a roll filled with meat, cheese, or egg salad, and lemon or chocolate dessert squares. Eloise told me she was a "bad" eater, and she ordered only a roll because she said she didn't eat "other people's soup." But she seemed to enjoy the outing, as did Arthur. The kind volunteers walked around filling and re-filling tea cups, and the room was alive with adults and children alike.

The people we'd met on Wednesday were there and greeted us like old friends. Ian and Gillian sat with us again. Jenny and her son sat at the next table and she kept apologizing for not sitting with us, saying, "You will be here next week right? We can catch up then," as if we actually lived here.

Joe and I chatted with everyone at our table and half the people at the next. We took pictures and saw widened eyes when I announced, just before taking the photo, that I'm writing a book about our adventures! Joe and I could clearly see ourselves living in this little village. We decided we would probably be volunteers serving food for the luncheons and would become goodwill ambassadors for the senior community here. Ian's wife gently took my arm and spelled out their last name, saying "We're in the phone book; stop by anytime." It took us almost as long to get out the door as it did for us to have lunch.

The four of us walked home through the grey drizzle to their house, where Eloise served up some hot tea and a plate of biscuits, though we'd just finished lunch a few minutes before. Soon after we began visiting, Lily and her husband arrived and were very surprised to find us there and to know that their parents had gone to the luncheon. Lily said she'd been trying to get them to go for ages, and she was so grateful to us. I told her it was just because we were pushy Americans. Besides we were strangers and they couldn't say no. The six of us talked for an hour or two and the afternoon flew by. Joe shared a lot of stories about Colorado and they were fascinated to hear of our life there. We laughed as I realized once again that we had enough stories for another book! We talked about our wedding and honeymoon combined, which we call our wedding-moon, our winter at the cowboy cabin outside of town on a 400-acre ranch in Colorado, our travels back and forth across the country, our adventures with bears, elk, bighorn sheep, and many other stories that have made up our last four years together in the great American West. To these two Scottish couples, the stories were entertaining to say the least.

Lily and George gave us a lift home so she could say a quick hello to Daisy. She told us she was glad that we were there taking care of Daisy, who has officially become the most spoiled cat on the planet.

A great day overall. Life gives you great times and challenges too, but the key is all in your perspective.

APRIL 3

George and Greenie Beanie

Yesterday was a cloudy day, both inside and out. We were both weary from staying up late making phone calls to home about Joe's dad, and from the subsequent discussions about ending our trip early. The decision was made, at least for now, that we would stay and practice the grace of doing nothing since there was nothing we could change by going back right now.

We spent the day mostly inside, resting and watching movies and being easy with ourselves. We got a loaf of freshly made focaccia bread from Main Street Bakery and made our own little pizzas. We watched movies and I fell asleep on the couch.

Today started off with much more promise. Though the weather was still cloudy, our moods were brighter, and we took an early walk with our Wellies on. We found a new footpath that led straight to the neighborhood golf course, and we managed to avoid getting clonked by a golf ball as we made our escape up the road. The course reminds me of one my Pappy used to take me on when he taught me how to golf. It was a chip and putt course on Route 422. If he were still here in human form, I'd love to take him golfing on this little course in Scotland.

We timed our walk to arrive back at the Main Street coffee shop just as the scones came out of the oven, which left no doubt in my mind that it would be a fresh scone for me and a tea, while Joe ordered his chocolate lovers' breakfast of hot chocolate and a brownie. To each his own. George came in for tea around the same time we did and sat at the table across from us, where we were lounging by the window on the leather couch.

George is an older man with long white hair and beard who wears a trench coat and shuffles his feet when he walks. He doesn't say hello or even seem to see us, but we've seen him all over the village and in the coffee shop almost every time we've been there. All the shopkeepers know him by name. He sat across from me, slurping his tea voraciously and I wondered what his story was. Was he homeless? Did he get tea there for free? Could I perhaps leave a few quid for him to get a scone with his tea the next time?

As we sat, the place filled up and a couple sat next to us at the high bar along one wall. We struck up a friendly banter about the crowdedness of the place and soon we were introducing ourselves. The man, whose name was Fadrice, was French and his wife was Scottish. I walked up to the counter to ask about George and when I returned Joe was busy telling them about this memoir I was writing about our adventures. Fadrice asked if the entries were online and could I send them for him to read. They suggested a few places for us to visit, including Melrose, which is where they live, and we could see that our week was going to be pretty full.

When I asked at the counter about George, the woman named Susan told me that George had been a top executive of some sort in the business world till one day he just stopped. She said people came in all the time buying him drinks, not knowing that he is really very wealthy. He lives on his own but has caretakers who come in to help him out and give him his medicine. I commented on the fact that the community seems to look after him, and she said yes, they absolutely do. Susan said, "It used to be George and Greenie Beanie, but now it's just George." I asked who Greenie Beanie was.

"Greenie Beanie was a woman with similar issues to George who the community also looked after," she said. "Everyone did. But then she started losing weight and got sick and now she lives in a nursing home." Why the name, I asked. Well, because, she said, she always wore a green beanie.

Joe and I got lucky later in the afternoon when the sun decided to come out for a bit and we were spurred on to take another walk. It's light until 8 p.m. now so it's hard to sit here and burn daylight. This time we walked back to my favorite "desk" by the water, and I sat for a bit while Joe scouted the area for interesting feathers or rocks. Joe always has his eyes to the ground.

We arrived home well-walked and ready to bring the evening in with a call to Joe's mom and some quality time with Daisy cat.

APRIL 8

Parallel lives

The days here have a strange rhythm to them. I realize my time is matched somewhat by things that are happening back home; my heart is there and my physical self is here, and I am learning a very important lesson about being present and giving my worries to God. Once more I literally see myself handing them over. It is a time of transition; I have felt transition on each sit as it drew toward its conclusion, but this time it is different.

I have a very best friend who is sick right now and I don't know how it is going to turn out. No one really ever does. All I know is that ever since I found out, I have had a hard time thinking of anything else. It's not even as if I am so worried about her, because I know her and I know she will be fine. If anyone has the strength to persevere physically, and most important, spiritually, she does. But I "feel" her all the time. Sometimes I think I feel her pain. My life seems to be on parallel with hers right now in some strange way.

I am doing very different things from her right now. She is resting, she is trying to eat, she is getting through the days and building her internal strength, I imagine, for what lies ahead. Me, I am waking up slowly, sleeping later, starting the day with Reiki for myself and for her, feeling somewhat melancholy in the mornings, but then slowly rising to greet the new day.

And I am greeting it with reverence and gratitude—gratitude for the sun or the clouds, for the man by my side, the kitty by my feet, a warm house, and good friends who are far away. I walk, with Joe by my side. I walk and walk alongside the River Tweed, on St. Cuthbert's Way.

This is the footpath where Joe continues to find white feathers—tiny soft white feathers that look like they came from the wings of a cherub. By no coincidence, our new friend Arthur (our homeowner's dad) hands Joe the newspaper with an article about white feathers, saying they are messages from the angels.

I'm quite sure the messages are for Joe about his dad, letting him know that everything is already all right, and for me about my best friend, letting me know that she is with me every step of the way as I am with her. As I walk, I imagine her with me, enjoying the sound of the river, the singing of many birds, the budding flowers and trees, and the walk itself: twisting and winding over bridges, along little creeks, through woods. I feel her with me on muddy paths where our Wellies squish and slide, past the spot where we saw the otter, to the chain link bridge where we cross to Dryburgh Abbey and the fields beyond, or the other direction to the donkey sanctuary.

I know that right now I must be fully present where I am, living fully for my friend and for me together. I'm happy to know her and relieved that she has shared with me what she is going through right now so I can send her love and Reiki. I wouldn't want it any other way. As she would tell me, all is in perfect order as it should be.

For this and several other reasons, I am being asked to prepare my Spirit for the times ahead. And I will look back on these days of quiet times and writing and walking and making new friends and draw strength from them. I am being called to cherish these days here; to cherish every day and every person in my life, both present and unseen, and to hone a vibration that flows to everyone I love right now. To wrap my loving arms around the Universe and give it a heart hug to ease its pain.

Our kind friends Lily and George took us to the seaside on Tuesday, this time to St. Abbs, which lies north of Berwick-upon-Tweed. The coastline is reminiscent of our time in Devon, hills springing up along the shoreline with walking paths from one village to the next.

George offered to drive the car around to the next beach so we could have a "wee" walk along the hilly coastline. Lily, wearing a boot due to a broken foot, could walk, but not too far. The day was cloudy and cold, but what a grand walk we had anyway.

George took pictures at every opportunity, mostly of us, and promised to share them once he figured out how to get them off his camera and onto their computer. We drove onto Eyemouth, where we had lunch. On the way home, George took us to Scott's View, a place where Sir Walter Scott went every day, presumably by horse and carriage, to look at the grand view of the mountains and valley below.

Several memorial plates talked about him; one said that on the day of his funeral, a procession at least a mile long came up that road and the horses stopped just beside what is now Scott's View, because they were used to stopping there each day with him in the carriage.

From there, we went on to see the great statue on the hill that Joe and I had been looking up at from across the river. Turned out the statue was of William Wallace, the man portrayed in the movie "Braveheart." William Wallace was a 13th century knight who fought for independence of Scotland from England and is known as one of its greatest heroes.[19]

Memorable walks and a visit to Kelso filled in our days. In Kelso, we found Caroline's coffee shop. Once we entered, a young woman told us we'd just walked into the best coffee shop in the Borders and she recommended the scones. I've come to appreciate a good scone here in Scotland. The secret seems to be in the flakiness. It helps greatly to have them fresh out of the oven. I've become quite fond of going into our village to the "famous" coffee shop and bookstore just in time for fresh scones at 10 a.m. and a pot of tea. I've since found that the owner of this shop used to be an editor for J.K. Rowling! So yesterday I decided to take myself there while Joe relaxed on the couch and do some writing, Rowling style!

I bought a new journal since my original one was full (thank goodness for my laptop!) and ordered a pot of Rooibos tea and a slice of carrot cake.

---

19 "William Wallace Biography," BIO, www.biography.com/people/william-wallace-9522479.

The cake only served to distract me, but it was a delicious distraction at that. The shop was busy, and I ended up sharing my table with another couple. They probably thought I was rude for writing and not talking. George, the local man who was always about, sat behind me on the couch. He seems to like hanging out in the coffee shop too.

I can't help thinking about what a perfect place that Great Spirit has taken us to. The Scottish Borders, it has been said by many, is one of the most beautiful parts of Scotland, and it certainly has some of the dearest people living here. The village is charming, as we were reminded today when we attended our Friday meet and greet lunch at the church hall. We sat with our now old friends Gillian and Jenny, and our newer friends Pam and Barbara. This time the question was "how was your week?" since we'd lunched together last Friday and there was now a sense of continuity. On our walk this morning, we saw a man we talked to before on the same path to the desk along the river and later saw another woman who is a neighbor on the way to the village. If we stayed here another month, we would become regulars for sure.

Jenny almost looked teary when we left with great hugs all around, saying we must come back again. And if we could manage it, there's still coffee this Saturday morning. She'd love for us to join the group once more.

But tomorrow is my dear friend Amy's visit (Amy is a friend I met in Sedona, Arizona who lives in Aberdeen, Scotland), a long-awaited one, so we won't make it to have coffee at the church. But we will think of them all fondly as we travel forward. And who knows, maybe we shall come back to the Borders again one day.

APRIL 9

Important discoveries

Amy's visit to us this weekend was intended to be a retreat time for her—a time to be away from her busy life as a healer in Aberdeen. And it was. She really enjoyed her time with us and all that we shared: the conversations, the meals, the walks, and our time together with Reiki.

It was also a very healing time for me. I felt the things she said allowed me to look more deeply at myself and see some things more clearly. A few things she said were direct messages for me. There was no doubt.

She talked about being approached by a ghostwriter to write a book. She told me she wasn't interested because in order for her to write a book, it would have to first have an intent, a purpose. She wouldn't want to publish a book just for the sake of being published. This made me look differently at this travel book I am writing. My ego, my ability to push things forward and get them out there, says *publish*. But after what Amy said, it made me reconsider. Yes, I want to write and publishing might be an option for me to get out a message. But what is that message? What is truly important, what do I want to give to the world? The answer that came was an awareness of Reiki, of the Light within us all and the wonder of travel and all it brings.

Our visit was so filled with constant sharing. Amy is a remarkable woman with many precious gifts that she brings to this world. She is a Reiki Master and a gifted animal communicator. In fact, she spoke with Daisy while she was with us.

That afternoon, as we all sat around the dining room table talking, with Daisy sitting quietly on a chair nearby, Amy looked at me and asked, "Does Daisy know about Hero's death?" I was absolutely stunned. It was as if someone had taken me and the binoculars through which I view the world and turned us 180 degrees to see something entirely different. Suddenly I saw the world close-up from Daisy's perspective. Of course she had a right to know what had happened to her brother! Why is it that we can live with animals and not acknowledge them in this way?

With that new awareness, I shook my head dumbly, feeling suddenly ashamed that I hadn't even thought of it. Amy wasn't judging me, though. She just asked, in her gentle way, if she could talk with Daisy, to which I said yes please. Once Amy opened up the conversation with Daisy (a silent conversation between her and Daisy) the first thing that Daisy said was to please thank us for taking such good care of her. She told Amy that she felt as if we were part of her pack, as it were. Then she asked how long her owners would be gone. No one had told her how long or when or even if they would be back. I know that animals understand us and know what we are saying, and I also know how much many of us overlook that. It's somewhat the same with adults and kids, you know.

Amy reassured Daisy that her "parents" would be back in a few days. Then she asked Daisy if she knew about Hero. Daisy did not, so Amy told her. Daisy said she thought he'd just gone off somewhere, especially since she'd seen me looking out the window a lot. She said that Hero was kind of wild and had caused Harriet and Bob some trouble. Say what you will, but this cat lives with them and of course she knows what's going on! She said she was a little worried about us because we seemed kind of stressed, and we were, over Hero. But overall she was really happy to be with us and very relaxed.

On Saturday, we met Amy's friend Beth for lunch at our now-familiar coffee shop. Beth and Amy used to work together with equine-assisted therapy for children. Afterward, Amy, Joe, and I talked away most of the afternoon at home and then decided to go get some fish and chips for dinner. I made us a spinach, roasted beet, and goat cheese salad to go along with the fish and chips. After dinner, we picked up where we had left off and talked some more before giving it up to go to sleep.

We picked up the conversation the next morning at breakfast and again, it was mainly centered on healing. I found that Amy's wisdom extends far beyond her years on this planet. She was guided as a very young woman to become a medium and work with angels. She spent the next 10 years or so learning healing on many levels. She hears and sees a lot and takes her gifts to help others quite seriously.

She pointed out in her gentle way that everything is made of love. Everything. This morning I realized that in order for me to be love, to embody love with my entire being, I have to let go of fear completely. And beyond that, I still have to open my heart more fully than I could ever dream of. It must be wide open all the time—as wide as the Grand Canyon—as deep as the deepest part of the ocean. And then some more.

My new intention is this: "I open my heart. I fear no more." We talked a lot about how fear replaces love for us as humans all the time, in every moment. One of her mentors says that when people talk about having to "let go" of control, he says, "we are all moving toward our death. What is there to hold onto?"

Why hold on at all? Let go into love.

There are many more things that will come through from this visit. It has been a true blessing, in fact, a real life miracle. Much gratitude to Amy.

APRIL 12

Don't be daft

What started out here in the Borders as potentially a difficult time, with me feeling lousy for some unknown reason, and then the death of Hero the cat, has turned out to be a time of continual discovery and the building of warm-hearted friendships, ones that won't easily be forgotten. The friendship and kindness we have been shown on this journey have woven their way throughout the entire month here and knowing this affirms my belief in the goodness of the human heart.

First there were Arthur and Eloise, Harriet's parents, who extended friendship. Then there were the few couples we met at the coffee shop and, following Hero's death, we came to know Lily and George, Harriet's sister and brother-in-law. They have been so kind about Hero's death—bringing us flowers and offering consolation, taking us to the seaside and buying us a meal, and giving us a ride to the train tomorrow. They also invited us to lunch for our last full day here.

When I tell them that they do too much, they say, "Don't be daft." What a great expression. To us Americans, it might sound like a rude thing to say, but when these lovely Scottish people say it, it makes you smile and know there's no arguing with them.

I love these two. It's as if we were guests in their country, coming to visit instead of doing a "job," as it were. They gave us the sense that they wanted to look after us and make sure we were having a good stay.

Today when I was speaking to Lily at lunch, she said, "Please come back to visit, and when you do, you must stay with us or my parents or with Harriet. I'll be upset if I hear you are staying in a hotel. I really mean it."

It's funny but in a way I think Hero's death brought us closer together. If it hadn't happened we might not have seen much of them, but the fact that it did happen created a link between us that would not be ignored. It took us beyond the formalities of strangers and into a deeper relationship. How blessed are we.

Arthur and Eloise picked us up today and took us to Earlston, where Lily and George live. I felt at home as soon as we arrived. Joe was joking with Lily and she was calling him "Cheeky Chops." This is an expression that suits Joe right down to the ground, as they say. He is so a Cheeky Chops, and he gets a laugh for it, with the right person, that is. Lily found him funny and delightful and he rose to the occasion!

Eloise really seemed to like me, and she took me by the hand, asking if I would like a house tour. Lily and George's home was just beautiful and quite large by my standards. The room where we sat had big windows at the back that looked out to a very large garden. It reminded me of a park with a high hedge at the back, and the mountains just visible beyond. I would be in heaven with that garden to daydream in. We joked as though we'd known each other for years, and Lily said we should move there, as we were good for them—with Joe making everyone laugh. I told everyone how Joe was picking up Scottish expressions like saying "aye" all the time. After that, Arthur, George and Eloise began to say aye after every sentence until we all burst into laughter.

Lunch was great. Lily had bought several ready-made dishes from the well-known Marks and Spencer but not the macaroni and cheese, which she had prepared herself. She joked, saying that the mac and cheese was the only thing that might not be safe to eat! Of course, that was the first thing both Joe and I went for and it was delicious. She'd bought a chocolate log for dessert. Lunch and conversation lasted three hours and probably would have gone on longer if I hadn't gotten up to put on my scarf.

I got Lily's email address so that I could keep in touch, and Eloise said to send messages to her through Lily since she doesn't do email. They both gave us a present. Eloise gave me a scarf with owls on it (more owl medicine!) and a box of shortbread for our journey. Lily gave us a really neat burlap-type bag that used to be made locally— gifts from the heart. I felt as though we were the ones who should be giving, but it certainly is blessed to receive from such lovely people.

Earlier that afternoon, when I had a quiet moment with Lily, I told her about Amy's talk with Daisy and she was absolutely stunned. The information I passed on was dead accurate and she knew it. I think the experience opened her eyes to the validity of animal communication as much as it had confirmed my own. I told Lily that I would send her Amy's contact information in case Harriet wanted to contact her. She could connect with Hero on the other side as well and maybe find out something about his death.

When I think about Hero's passing and all the events surrounding it, I realize that I have gained some valuable insights that will have a positive effect on many parts of my life. One is that at the time of Hero's disappearance, I was not completely present and paying attention. I was relating to Hero as an independent cat but not connecting with him on a spiritual level where I might have "known" about his accident, maybe even before it happened. A key to this experience is what it has taught me about paying attention to those gut feelings more often and the importance of stepping back to see the bigger picture of what is happening in the here and now.

Second, Hero's death and Amy's visit and communication with Daisy have opened my eyes to the utter importance of animal communication. Speaking to animals and letting them speak to us can be of help to so many others, as it has been for Lily and Harriet, and Daisy, too. Suddenly, I feel a yearning to be able to hear what the animals that I come into contact with want to tell me. And with Reiki on my side and my mantra to "open my heart and fear no more," there are no limits. Thank you, Amy and thank you, Hero and Daisy. The lessons are magnificent.

April 13

Why am I so happy?

We have just left St. Boswell's to take the train to Edinburgh, and it already feels like a weight has been lifted. It's hard to explain. Was it the weight of carrying Hero around, unseen and unfelt, but somehow still there?

Suddenly, somehow, I am feeling free. Traveling through the grey day on a train crowded with commuters, I wear my headphones, listening to Julie True's "Your Love is Extravagant. I love Julie's music. It just makes me "smile in my liver" (more from *Eat, Pray, Love* when Ketut, the medicine man, tells Liz that when she meditates she must smile, even in her liver).

This sudden freedom comes alongside a recognition of lessons learned on this housesit and the words, the glorious free-flowing words, to describe those lessons. My fears were being tested there. Sick suddenly, unable to breathe, to digest. To digest life. Possibly an allergic reaction to the cats? Yes possibly. But where and how did it hit me? In my chest, my GI tract, my ability to digest life. Fear, swallowing fear.

And as if in answer, right now Julie is singing, "Stir up the love in my heart." Yessirrreee, stir up the love, stir it up, stir it up. I fear no more, because I am made of love.

Why am I so happy? I am a guest speaker on different Internet radio shows, where I talk about Reiki. My good friend and radio host Paula Vail has invited me to be a guest on her new show. It's literally called, "Why Am

I So Happy?" I have begun thinking about this title and what it means to me. I am so happy because I've realized, with the help of Reiki and its connection to Source, that ALL is love. Everything, everyone, every hurt, every leaf, every piece of trash on the street is love. Pollution is love. Cats are love. Bugs are love.

And so I can walk with joy and with love. I can move through every experience in my life, through pain, through the passing of loved ones and my own self, through slow traffic, through sleepless nights, all with pure joy, because I know now it is all Love.

My new mantra: *I am made of Love; I harbor NO fear.* Is this enlightenment? If it is, I invite it to stay. Why am I so happy? Because I live in love.

There is something so delightful about riding a train, especially through scenic Scotland. The train itself is so comforting as it glides on its track, carrying you along like when you were a child and were carried everywhere. Effortlessly, you go along for the ride, with big windows to watch the ever-changing scenery: the sheep, the green fields, and hills.

Or nap as Joe does now. Or just chat, as do the two young girls who sit beside us. It's a time to be suspended from the world.

Soon we will be back in the old city of Edinburgh. Now a familiar friend, its old buildings await, holding fast unto their magic until our return. I cannot wait to spend some time there, writing another book one day.

I don't know how or when it will happen but I know it will. I feel bursting with ideas for more books and joyous just thinking of it. Don't know why I waited so long to get there, but very glad I've arrived. She writes.

We've made good friends at our house-sit in St. Boswell in the Borders with Lily, George, Eloise and Arthur. Amy from Aberdeen has become a much closer friend to both of us as well as an inspiration! We didn't do anything during her stay except eat, walk, talk, and share Reiki, but every moment was full. She will be married and maybe we'll be invited to her "ceilidh." She says they may have a very small wedding, maybe even just the two of them, but small or not, they will have a ceilidh, where the men wear kilts and everyone dances the night away. So if we are invited, we must come back to Scotland!

It's later in the day now and I'm sitting here in a high-backed chair looking out toward the sea through one of the three bay windows of our sixth-floor hotel room. The water is shrouded in a grey mist that blends seamlessly into the overcast sky. I can imagine the sea life out there, the dolphins and the whales, the lobster and other fish. I can imagine on a sunny day I might see a sunset on that water, though I'm not sure which direction I'm looking at this moment.

Joe is curled up and napping on the large bed in our posh room. I took Lily's advice and it has worked out beautifully. She suggested I ask at the Scotsman Hotel for a room with a view, since it would be our last night in Scotland. I called ahead and did just that. And when we arrived at this grand hotel, where everyone treated us like we had diamonds dripping off our hands and a title after our names (instead of me with a hole in the heel of my boot), the lovely Katie at reception told us we'd been upgraded to a suite with a view.

We arrived at the hotel at half eleven, only to discover that our room would not be ready for a while but that the concierge would happily take our bags to our room when it was. In the meantime, with a wait ahead of us, Joe and I decided to—what else?—go for a walk in the drizzle of the day! I wanted to buy Joe what they call a drinking kilt. He hasn't bought anything for himself during the whole time we've been here except a new pair of shoes, and I think it would be perfect! He's letting me talk him into it (I think).

Eventually, hunger overtook us and after looking at menus for several places, I glanced up suddenly and saw the Elephant House, with a sign that said it was a place of inspiration for many of J.K. Rowling's early novels, which she wrote sitting in this coffeehouse.

We sat in the back room where she did a lot of writing and found a corner table where I would choose to sit and write. We ate sandwiches and each had a beer (well to be honest, I had two sips of a beer and Joe finished both of ours, hence the afternoon nap that ensued for him later), and I took loads of pictures of the elephants, which were everywhere—elephant paintings, posters, elephant models, statues, a chair carved like an elephant. I thought of my sister-in-law, who loves elephants.

We left and walked across the street to the National Museum. All the museums are free in Edinburgh, and this one was awe-inspiring with stuffed, life-sized animals of every kind: giraffe, tiger, lion, elephant.

Another section of the museum was filled with prayer flags, prayer wheels, and a huge totem pole.

With so many people and so many things to see, we got overwhelmed and ducked out into the fresh air. Back on the Royal Mile, Joe tried on a few kilts but wouldn't commit. I thought he looked pretty cute.

We headed back to the Scotsman, where we could now check in. The concierge showed us to our room. After our excursions this morning and earlier this afternoon, tonight we will have a wee snack in the hotel bar and enjoy a quiet night. But in the meantime, I stood looking out the window onto the street below where I could see (and hear) a man on the corner singing for his supper, tin cup on the ground in front of him, and at the same time watch a train disappear into a tunnel as it left Waverley Station. As I stood taking in our room and the view, I realized that never in my life would I have dreamt of staying in such a grand place, much less being in one of the most mystical cities in Europe. And then, with typical Rose-style irony, I switched from taking in the luxuriousness of our room to contemplating where we could get an inexpensive breakfast the next morning. Life is grand and altogether pretty funny too.

Despite the magic of our surroundings, I cannot help but think of Harriet, our homeowner who has arrived home to find that she is sadly minus one cat. Lily, Harriet's sister, thought it best that we not be there when they arrived home. She knew they would be devastated at the news of losing their dear Hero, which is why we left this morning. It felt awkward, as our instinct would be to offer a loving presence for these dear people who opened their homes to us, but we followed the kind advice of the family about the situation. We left them a nice card and a casserole of aubergine parmesan (now my signature dish) in the refrigerator, said goodbye to Miss Daisy, and boarded the train to Edinburgh. It is a strange irony that we are here, enjoying a beautiful night in a grand hotel, whilst they are at their home, adjusting to the shock of Hero's death. I am sending them love.

Yet in spite of all this, or perhaps in light of it, my job is to be in the moment, and in this moment I am feeling blissful about being in my dear Edinburgh once more. It was a special treat to be allowed one more night in this grand city of old. I asked Joe to promise that if he did not buy a kilt here today, he would get one if we come back for Amy's ceilidh. A proper drinking kilt. And there are only two things to do when you're wearing a drinking kilt: drink and dance. Dance all night long.

APRIL 15

From Edinburgh to Thirsk

I awoke to blue sky that expanded as the morning grew on Edinburgh. Always a beautiful city, it is absolutely breathtaking when it's framed by brilliant blue above the giant old structures and the sun lights up the corners and edges of it all.

We followed a leisurely wake-up with breakfast at La Locanda on Cockburn, a winding cobblestone street just around the corner from the

Scotsman. A very city-like coffee house, its tables sat close together with a bench seat that ran along one wall underneath high ceilings and below them on the walls, shelves of bottles full of beer, wine, Pellegrino, and cordials.

The Italian waiter/manager brought me my bowl of fruit, calling it Macedonia. When I looked puzzled, he laughed and said that it meant a bowl of mixed fruit. It was named after the country Macedonia because of the "mess" of different populations of people. He and Joe shared an easy camaraderie since Joe explained that he is learning what the Italian's call "dolce far niente," or the sweetness of doing nothing. Joe bragged that he is, in fact, retired, and doing nothing right now. His new Italian friend told him, "I cannot wait to be as old as you so I can do this."

I enjoyed a half croissant (saving the other half for the train) and my Macedonia. Croissants are one of my very favorite things. Joe dug into a full Scottish: organic egg, mushroom and sausage black pudding.

After a lovely if brief walk to savor a last look at the skyline from Princes Street and to video a man in full Scottish dress playing bagpipes, Joe went to look once more at the Sir Walter Scott memorial while I left a few coins for the bagpipe player and then also shared a few quid with a homeless person just a few yards on down the street.

Bye for now, Edinburgh. Until we meet again.

Later in the day, after a pleasant train ride, we landed in Thirsk, England. It was an unremarkable entrance, as there was no ticket machine, no station building, not even a place to stand out of the rain—just us with our many bags (they have a way of coming with us everywhere). Luckily, there was one man about the station, and he called a cab for us.

Once settled at the Kirkgate House B & B, we walked around town and found a proper pub that our host Jeff recommended called The Little 3's. Several of the locals welcomed us warmly and invited us to sit in their designated corner. They showered us with questions, mostly about where we'd been and where we were planning to go. Somehow I think that is an age-old question asked of travelers over all time.

Then they proceeded to tell us where we should go (namely—York) and what to see when we get there (for example, the pub that floods every time it rains, so much so that they have a measuring stick inside that shows the water marks). A woman named Ellie shared the news of her upcoming 70th birthday party to be held—you guessed it—here at the pub! She's been coming to this pub since she was 17. I imagine everybody knows her name!

The conversation turned pleasantly toward author James Herriot, since the real reason we are in Thirsk is to go to The World of James Herriot, a museum centered on the veterinarian's life here in this part of England. One of the men in our circle of new friends named Peter, who is a retired journalist, met James Herriot while doing a rare interview some years ago and said that Herriot was a very private man—so private, in fact, that when word was out that a load of fans were coming to town to see him, the farmers around the countryside would "hide" him by calling him out to their farms to tend to their animals.

It's funny to me that many people in the US don't even know who he is—the world's most famous veterinary surgeon. Herriot has entertained Joe and me with his stories and television shows for many hours, becoming like an old and dear friend to us. So hearing stories about the actual man when he was alive and living in Thirsk was, for me, like being told stories of someone in my own family.

When we visited his museum the next day, it was like bringing to life everything I ever read or saw or knew about the man. Every room of the house had been lovingly preserved and looked exactly like it did in the TV shows. You could almost see him running down the long hallways to the kitchen where his wife Helen was cooking breakfast or the surgery where he and his partner Siegfried saw their small animal patients. There were several buildings out back that have been set up as a tribute to a man who touched the lives of so many in his time. They even have a replica of the set that was used for the show, which depicted the 1930s and 40s. Herriot is as dear to me as Harry Potter is to millions of other people.

Not surprisingly, I was very intrigued with the information about James Herriot's writing habits. He wrote in his living room sitting across from Helen while the family watched TV. He wrote in short snippets (since that's all he had time for), capturing the stories that had accumulated like intricate cobwebs in his head over the years. Perhaps his needing to write in snippets is why each chapter is a story in itself, having a beginning, climax, and ending so that you are able to read his books "one snippet at a time."

Inspiring to me as a writer since he didn't begin writing until after age 50, his many books tell of his adventures as a vet in the Yorkshire Dales treating all creatures great and small. Many of those stories are laugh-aloud funny, some sad, others simply wonderfully memorable. He wrote with a straightforward style while making the people and places come alive for his reader. Joe and I have spent many a night in bed on a cold Colorado evening reading a chapter or two from his books and just laughing a lot. The museum is a family-created tribute to a great author, a kind man and a true animal lover.

This afternoon it's been chucking rain, and we shall have dinner again at the Little 3's where we ate last night. The first time we ate there, we each had one of their famous pies called the Heidi, a small delicacy made with perfectly crunchy crust with just the right amount of flakiness, and filled with sweet potato, goat cheese, onion sliced so thin you can barely see it, and spinach. It makes my mouth water just thinking of it.

Tomorrow, there will be the long train journey to London, then onto Northamptonshire to be reunited for a blink with young Henry, Nikki, and Alex before our flight home to the US! Archangel Raphael, patron saint of travelers, thank you for watching over us on our journey.

APRIL 20

Flying back to the USA

One afternoon not long after our courtship began, Joe looked into my eyes with a smile and asked, "Are you ready for the ride?" I said yes, yes I was and ever since then what a ride it has been. Our trip to the UK is one of many journeys he and I have taken together, and it has been a wonderful adventure that we will always cherish.

We have carried Reiki with us for these many months through the UK, going from town to town on trains, buses, cabs, and along the many footpaths. So naturally as we sat comfortably in the back row waiting for the plane to move. I began to ask Reiki to fill the cabin, to surround the pilots and crew and all the people flying.

Suddenly I got this nudge, telling me to send Reiki to the small parts of the plane. This was something I've never done before—given any thought to the mechanics of the plane. I've always surrounded the whole plane in Light, but this message was so specific. I didn't question it; I just started to focus on the underneath of the plane and its mechanisms.

A few minutes later we were still sitting there and the pilot's voice came on. He announced that we would be taking off in just a few minutes, but that first they had to check on a minor mechanical difficulty. Astounding! Such a direct message from the Divine, intuitively guiding us at all times.

APRIL 22

I am here to learn

I have, since I was a little girl, consciously or unconsciously chosen to lead a deeply spiritual life. Once you choose to bring Reiki in to your life, it changes you in so many ways, pushing you further along that spiritual path. It changes who you are, deep down to the core. Reiki has a way of bringing up the things that are not so nice about you, making you look at them and asking if you want to heal them. It makes you look at your habits and asks you to change the ones that are not in alignment with Reiki. You may try to go back to your old ways, but it feels hollow and your vibration doesn't like it. Reiki calls you to be the best person in this life that you can be. It lets you know when you aren't doing that—not in a gruff way, but in a most loving and kind way. Reiki guides, ever so gently and ever so powerfully, if we but ask.

On this magical journey, Reiki asked me to stretch myself in new ways, to learn more about who I am in this life, and to seek to know more of my Authentic Self. I have filled these pages about our experiences, and those experiences always, in some way or another, inevitably led back to Reiki. What I found on this trip was that I *am* Reiki at the core of it all. We all are.

Reiki protected us and guided us throughout all the months we traveled from place to place and house to house. We never had any fear or even any thought of getting lost or hurt. To the contrary, that loving energy brought wonderful, caring people into our lives wherever we went.

Throughout this trip I found a renewed sense of spirituality that had nothing to do with the outside world. I found more joy in my surroundings, rain or sun, warm or cold, comfortable or challenging. I learned to have more respect for giving myself time to do the things that are important to me, and with that, discovered more compassion and love for myself, often the hardest thing of all. I dug deep and found that my own opinion of myself could be pretty harsh and judgmental, and I asked Reiki's love to help me begin to heal those wounds against myself. I realized with startling clarity that every single thought I had against myself carried a vibration that affected the entire world. I found a deepening connection to the Divine Consciousness that links us all.

As Joe and I move forward, heads held high, walking into the abyss, I don't know where we will live or what our future will bring. But there is one thing I do know---as long as I am grounded in and surrounded by Reiki, I am home.

Author's Note

If you love the footpaths of the UK as much as we have, please consider connecting with the following organization who does much to help preserve them.

The Ramblers is the UK's largest walking charity. We are dedicated to defending walkers' rights, maintaining and improving paths, and protecting the places we all love to walk so that everyone, everywhere can discover the joys of walking.

We believe everyone deserves to right to experience the benefits of walking. If you do too, you can support us at www.ramblers.org.uk/donate or join our walking community as a member at www.ramblers.org.uk/join or by calling our friendly Supporter Care Team on 020 3961 3232.

Acknowledgements

To Hero, for teaching us what a true hero was. Thank you for the lessons you allowed us to learn.

To all the homeowners who opened up their homes and their hearts to us and allowed us to share this story with you. Though we changed your names here for your privacy, you stay engraved on our hearts. We have felt honored to stay in your home and be entrusted with the care of your beloved animals.

To all the people who welcomed us as friends – we shall not forget our time together.

To all the animals with whom we had the true honor of sharing time and learning lessons from, we thank you humbly and with heart. Tigger and Roo, Molly and Biscuit, Mufasa, Sarafina and the chickens, Ella, and Hero and Daisy. You enriched our lives and gave us pure love.

To my BF Nikki and our entire UK family, for giving me a reason to come to the UK and for always being there for me, through thick and through thin.

To Tara Flanagan, for your insight and editing support and your friendship, I am truly grateful.

To Rachel Bostwick, for her creative cover design, you are an inspiration.

To Rosie Pearson, for helping me bring this together in such a beautiful way, I thank you for your wonderful editing and your loving guidance.

To Sharon, a friend who loves me and really sees me. That is a true gift.

And most of all to Larry, without whom this book never would have been born.

About the Author

Rose O'Connor is a Reiki teacher and practitioner, writer, nature nut, and avid walker who loves finding new footpaths in life. She is busy at work on her newest fiction novel set in Ireland. She and her husband never tire of seeing new places and she hopes your journey with them is a pleasant experience. You can contact her via her email: rose@reikislove.com

Footpaths is her first book.

Made in the USA
Middletown, DE
07 December 2021